UK RENAL DIET COOKBOOK FOR BEGINNERS

UK EDITION

Quick and Easy Delicious Recipes Low in Sodium, Phosphorus and Potassium to Manage Your Kidney Disease in UK.

Grab Your Freebie
Download the e-book
Kidney-Friendly Recipes for UK Festivities
from this link:
https://drive.google.com/file/d/1fWchs-QDwDLwrlVCx2rOp6ugCOP5hR-A/view?usp=sharing

Roger Dash

Table of contents

- Table of contents 2
- Introduction 7
  - What is Nephropathy (Kidney Disease): 7
  - Types of Kidney Disease: 7
  - 5 Simple Steps to Slow Down Nephropathy: 9
  - Why Maintain an Adequate Water Balance? 10
  - What to Eat at The Restaurant: 11
  - Shopping List: 11
  - What to Eat: 11
  - What to Avoid: 12
  - Eating in England and Kidney Problems: 13
- Chapter 1. Breakfast Recipes 14
  - COLD RECIPES 14
    1. AVOCADO AND TOMATO RICE CAKES .. 14
    2. COTTAGE CHEESE AND BERRY BOWL ... 14
    3. FRUIT SALAD 14
    4. GREEK YOGURT AND HONEY PARFAIT . 15
    5. MARMALADE AND TOAST 15
    6. SCONE AND BUTTER 15
    7. SIMPLE FRUIT PARFAIT 16
    8. TEACAKE AND JAM 16
    9. WHOLEMEAL TOAST WITH MARMITE .. 17
    10. YOGURT AND GRANOLA 17
  - HOT RECIPES 17
    11. AVOCADO TOAST 17
    12. BANANA PANCAKES 18
    13. BEAN AND CHEESE TOASTIE 18
    14. BRAN MUFFINS 19
    15. CHEESE AND TOMATO TOASTIE 19
    16. CINNAMON TOAST 19
    17. CRUMPETS AND JAM 20
    18. EGG AND SPINACH WRAP 20
    19. EGGS BENEDICT 21
    20. ENGLISH MUFFIN WITH COTTAGE CHEESE AND CUCUMBER 21
    21. FULL ENGLISH BREAKFAST 22
    22. GRILLED TOMATOES AND MUSHROOMS 22
    23. PORRIDGE 23
    24. RICE PUDDING 23
    25. SCRAMBLED EGGS AND TOAST 23
    26. SMOKED HADDOCK AND POACHED EGG 24
    27. SMOKED SALMON AND CREAM CHEESE BAGEL 24
    28. TOAST AND BAKED BEANS 25
    29. TOAST WITH EGG AND ASPARAGUS 25
    30. VEGETABLE BREAKFAST HASH 26
    31. VEGGIE OMELETTE 26
    32. WHOLEMEAL MUFFINS 26
  - SMOOTHIES 27
    33. APPLE AND OAT SMOOTHIE 27
    34. BERRY BLAST SMOOTHIE 27
    35. BLUEBERRY-BANANA SMOOTHIE 28
    36. CARROT-ORANGE SMOOTHIE 28
    37. CUCUMBER-MINT REFRESHER 28
    38. GREEN POWER JUICE 29
    39. MELON MINT COOLER 29
    40. ORANGE SUNRISE SMOOTHIE 29
    41. PAPAYA-COCONUT SMOOTHIE 30
    42. PEACH-GINGER SMOOTHIE 30

43. PINEAPPLE-SPINACH SMOOTHIE 30
44. STRAWBERRY-BANANA SHAKE 31
45. TROPICAL DELIGHT SMOOTHIE........ 31
46. KIWI-SPINACH SMOOTHIE 32
47. WATERMELON-MINT SMOOTHIE 32

APPLE AND OAT SMOOTHIES 32
48. CLASSIC APPLE AND OAT SMOOTHIE 32
49. APPLE, BEET, AND OAT SMOOTHIE..33
50. APPLE, CARROT, AND GINGER OAT SMOOTHIE 33
51. APPLE, PEAR, AND OAT SMOOTHIE .33
52. SPICED APPLE AND OAT SMOOTHIE 34
53. APPLE, MINT, AND CUCUMBER OAT SMOOTHIE 34
54. SCOTTISH APPLE AND BARLEY OAT SMOOTHIE 34

Chapter 2. Main Courses Recipes 36
MEAT DISHES 36
55. BEEF AND VEGETABLE STEW........... 36
56. CHICKEN AND LEEK PIE 36
57. CORNED BEEF HASH......................... 36
58. CUMBERLAND SAUSAGE 37
59. HAGGIS.. 37
60. ROAST BEEF.. 38
61. SHEPHERD'S PIE 38
62. STEAK AND KIDNEY PIE 38
63. TOAD IN THE HOLE........................... 39
64. YORKSHIRE PUDDING WITH BEEF 39

FISH DISHES 40
65. BAKED COD WITH HERB CRUST 40
66. FISH AND CHIPS 40
67. GRILLED MACKEREL 40
68. HADDOCK CHOWDER....................... 41
69. KEDGEREE 41
70. LEMON BAKED SALMON 42
71. POACHED HADDOCK WITH DILL SAUCE 42
72. SCOTTISH FISH PIE............................ 42
73. SMOKED SALMON SALAD 43
74. SOLE MEUNIÈRE................................ 43

VEGETARIAN DISHES... 43
75. BAKED STUFFED PEPPERS 44
76. CAULIFLOWER STEAK 44
77. CHEESY VEGETABLE CASSEROLE 44
78. CHICKPEA CURRY 45
79. EGGPLANT PARMESAN 45
80. LENTIL STEW 45
81. MUSHROOM RISOTTO 46
82. QUINOA AND VEGETABLE STIR-FRY .46
83. RATATOUILLE 47
84. VEGETABLE PAELLA 47

Chapter 3. BONUS. Air Fryer Main Courses........... 48
MEAT DISHES 48
85. AIR FRYER ROAST CHICKEN 48
86. AIR FRYER BEEF STEAK 48
87. AIR FRYER PORK CHOPS 48
88. AIR FRYER LAMB KEBABS 49
89. AIR FRYER TURKEY MEATBALLS 49
90. AIR FRYER DUCK BREASTS................ 50
91. AIR FRYER CORNISH HEN 50
92. AIR FRYER VENISON STEAKS 50
93. AIR FRYER RABBIT LEGS 51
94. AIR FRYER MEATLOAF 51

FISH DISHES 52

- 95. AIR FRYER TROUT WITH ALMONDS .52
- 96. AIR FRYER LEMON SOLE 52
- 97. AIR FRYER HERBED COD 52
- 98. AIR FRYER HERB-CRUSTED HADDOCK 53
- 99. AIR FRYER SEABASS WITH GARLIC AND LIME 53
- 100. AIR FRYER PLAICE WITH CAPERS 54
- 101. AIR FRYER SOLE IN PARCHMENT 54
- 102. AIR FRYER SALMON WITH DILL SAUCE 54
- 103. AIR FRYER SCOTTISH KIPPERS WITH OAT CRUST 55
- 104. AIR FRYER MACKEREL WITH HERB MARINADE 55

VEGETARIAN DISJES 56
- 105. AIR FRYER STUFFED MUSHROOMS ..56
- 106. AIR FRYER SWEET POTATO CAKES ...56
- 107. AIR FRYER CHEESY CAULIFLOWER ...57
- 108. AIR FRYER BUTTERNUT SQUASH FRIES 57
- 109. AIR FRYER BRUSSELS SPROUTS WITH BALSAMIC 57
- 110. AIR FRYER BEETROOT CHIPS 58
- 111. AIR FRYER GARLIC HERB ZUCCHINI ..58
- 112. AIR FRYER STUFFED BELL PEPPERS ..58
- 113. AIR FRYER ASPARAGUS SPEARS 59
- 114. AIR FRYER TOMATO AND BASIL BRUSCHETTA 59

Chapter 4. Vegetable side dishes, salads 61
VEGETABLE SIDE DISHES 61
- 115. ROASTED PARSNIPS WITH THYME ...61
- 116. BUTTERED PEAS WITH MINT 61
- 117. SCOTTISH NEEPS AND TATTIES 61
- 118. BRAISED RED CABBAGE 62
- 119. GRILLED LEEKS WITH VINAIGRETTE .62
- 120. CELERIAC MASH 63
- 121. ROASTED SWEDE WITH ROSEMARY 63
- 122. BUTTERED KALE WITH NUTMEG 63
- 123. MINTED PEAS AND CARROTS 64
- 124. BALSAMIC GLAZED BRUSSELS SPROUTS 64

VEGETABLE SALADS 65
- 125. BEETROOT AND ORANGE SALAD 65
- 126. WATERCRESS AND PEAR SALAD 65
- 127. RADISH AND CUCUMBER SALAD 65
- 128. ROASTED VEGETABLE SALAD 66
- 129. PEA AND MINT SALAD 66
- 130. CABBAGE AND APPLE SALAD 67
- 131. CARROT AND CORIANDER SALAD 67
- 132. SPRING GREENS SALAD 68
- 133. TOMATO AND BASIL SALAD 68
- 134. ASPARAGUS AND LEMON SALAD 69

Chapter 5: Hot & Cold Starters 70
HOT STARTERS 70
GRILLED STARTERS 70
- 135. GRILLED AUBERGINE ROLLS 70
- 136. GRILLED COURGETTE AND PEPPER SKEWERS 70
- 137. GRILLED ASPARAGUS WITH LEMON ZEST 71
- 138. GRILLED PORTOBELLO MUSHROOMS 71

SOUP STARTERS 72
- 139. LEEK AND POTATO SOUP 72
- 140. PEA AND MINT SOUP 72
- 141. CARROT AND CORIANDER SOUP 73

| 142. | CREAMY CAULIFLOWER SOUP 73
| 143. | ROASTED TOMATO SOUP 74

FRIED STARTERS..74
- 144. BLACK PUDDING BONBONS 74
- 145. SPICED PARSNIP FRITTERS 75
- 146. FRIED VEGETABLE BALLS.................75
- 147. FRIED SWEET POTATO WEDGES 76
- 148. MINI SCOTCH EGGS..........................76
- 149. BUBBLE AND SQUEAK CAKES 77

BAKED STARTERS 77
- 150. MINI TOAD IN THE HOLE.................77
- 151. WELSH RAREBIT BITES 78
- 152. CORNISH PASTY BITES.....................78
- 153. MINI SHEPHERD'S PIES....................79
- 154. MUSHROOM AND SPINACH TARTLETS 79

COLD STARTERS 80

SEAFOOD STARTERS 80
- 155. SMOKED SALMON AND DILL BITES ..80
- 156. SHRIMP COCKTAIL..........................80
- 157. CRAB AND AVOCADO TARTARE 81
- 158. TUNA AND CUCUMBER CUPS 81
- 159. SMOKED MACKEREL PÂTÉ 81

SALAD STARTERS 82
- 160. ROCKET AND PEAR SALAD 82
- 161. CUCUMBER AND RADISH SALAD......82
- 162. TOMATO AND BASIL SALAD 83
- 163. BEETROOT AND FETA SALAD 83
- 164. MIXED BERRY AND SPINACH SALAD 84

VEGETABLE STARTERS 84
- 165. STUFFED CHERRY TOMATOES..........84
- 166. CUCUMBER AND AVOCADO ROLLS..85
- 167. BELL PEPPER AND HUMMUS CUPS ..85
- 168. GRILLED VEGETABLE ANTIPASTO.....85
- 169. ZUCCHINI RIBBONS WITH LEMON ...86

MEAT AND CHEESE STARTERS 86
- 170. PROSCIUTTO AND MELON BITES 86
- 171. TURKEY AND CHEESE ROLL-UPS.......87
- 172. BEEF AND BLUE CHEESE CROSTINI...87
- 173. HAM AND CREAM CHEESE ROLL-UPS 88
- 174. CHICKEN AND AVOCADO SALAD CUPS 88
- 175. MINI CAPRESE SKEWERS 88

Chapter 6: Soup 90
- 176. SCOTTISH BARLEY SOUP 90
- 177. ENGLISH PEA AND HAM SOUP.........90
- 178. LENTIL AND VEGETABLE SOUP.........91
- 179. BROCCOLI AND CHEDDAR SOUP......91
- 180. CREAMY PARSNIP SOUP...................92
- 181. TOMATO AND LENTIL SOUP.............92
- 182. CARROT AND GINGER SOUP 93
- 183. LEEK AND SPINACH SOUP 93
- 184. CREAMY CELERY SOUP....................94
- 185. PUMPKIN AND SAGE SOUP 94

Chapter 7: Sweets and Snacks............................96

BAKED SWEETS 96
- 186. APPLE AND CINNAMON MUFFINS ...96
- 187. LEMON BLUEBERRY SCONES...........96
- 188. RASPBERRY OAT BARS 97
- 189. PEAR AND GINGER LOAF.................98
- 190. BANANA BREAD 98
- 191. ALMOND BISCOTTI..........................99
- 192. CARROT CAKE SQUARES 100

CAKES..100

- 193. CLASSIC VICTORIA SPONGE CAKE ..100
- 194. LEMON DRIZZLE CAKE 101
- 195. CHOCOLATE BEETROOT CAKE 102
- 196. ORANGE POLENTA CAKE 102
- 197. COCONUT LIME CAKE 103
- 198. BERRY YOGURT CAKE 104
- 199. GINGERBREAD CAKE 104

COOKIES 105
- 200. OATMEAL RAISIN COOKIES 105
- 201. CHOCOLATE CHIP COOKIES............106
- 202. LEMON SUGAR COOKIES................106
- 203. PEANUT BUTTER COOKIES 107
- 204. ALMOND BISCOTTI........................108

SAVORY SNACKS 108
- 205. ROSEMARY CHICKPEA CRISPS 109
- 206. BAKED ZUCCHINI CHIPS 109
- 207. SPICED SWEET POTATO WEDGES ..110
- 208. HERB-CRUSTED CAULIFLOWER BITES 111
- 209. CHEESE AND CHIVE POPCORN 111

Chapter 8: British Drinks for Renal Well-being....113
- 210. ENGLISH ELDERFLOWER SPRITZER.113
- 211. CUCUMBER MINT COOLER 113
- 212. BRITISH BERRY FIZZ 114
- 213. GINGER APPLE REFRESHER 114
- 214. CITRUS HERBAL ICED TEA.............114
- 215. MINT AND LIME SPARKLER 115
- 216. LOW-ALCOHOL PIMM'S CUP.........115
- 217. RENAL-FRIENDLY GIN AND TONIC..116
- 218. WHISKY AND GINGER...................116
- 219. LAVENDER LEMONADE 116
- 220. STRAWBERRY BASIL MOCKTAIL 117
- 221. SPICED APPLE MOCKTAIL..............117

Cooking Strategies 119
  Low-Sodium Cooking Techniques..................119
  Reducing Phosphorus and Potassium............119
  General Tips 120
More Tips for Eating Out 120
  Common Dishes in British Restaurants 120
  Strategies for Eating Out 121
INDEX..122

Introduction

What is Nephropathy (Kidney Disease):

Diabetic nephropathy, a type of chronic kidney disease (CKD), emerges when the kidneys, which regulate fluid and salt levels in the body and play a pivotal role in controlling blood pressure and cardiovascular health, are affected by high blood sugar levels resulting from diabetes. This condition can be observed in individuals with type 1, type 2, or gestational diabetes, which arises during pregnancy and increases the risk of type 2 diabetes later in life.

Diabetes disrupts the body's ability to produce or utilise insulin properly, leading to elevated glucose levels that gradually damage various parts of the body, including the cardiovascular system and kidneys. This damage, specifically termed diabetic nephropathy, is a major cause of long-term kidney disease and end-stage renal disease (ESRD). In ESRD, the kidneys can no longer meet daily life requirements, potentially leading to kidney failure with severe consequences.

Nephropathy can affect individuals with any type of diabetes, as it stems from damage caused by high blood glucose levels. The kidneys, responsible for filtering blood from the body's arteries, are adversely affected by elevated blood glucose levels.

According to a 2016 study, 20-40% of people with diabetes develop some form of kidney disease. Diagnostic tests may reveal the following indicators:

- High levels of albumin in the urine: Healthy kidneys should not contain any albumin protein in the urine.
- Low glomerular filtration rate (GFR): The kidneys' primary function is to filter blood, and kidney damage impairs this process. Ideally, the kidneys should function at 100% or have a GFR of 100. A GFR of 60% or higher does not indicate kidney disease, while a range of 15-60% is indicative of kidney disease. A GFR below 15% signifies kidney failure.

ESRD represents the final stage of kidney disease, with diabetic nephropathy being the leading cause of ESRD cases in the United States. Approximately 40-50% of ESRD cases are linked to diabetes, necessitating dialysis for individuals with ESRD.

Managing blood sugar levels effectively can reduce the risk of developing diabetic nephropathy:
Whether a person has type 1 or type 2 diabetes, they can mitigate the risk by:

- Monitoring and maintaining blood glucose levels within the target range.
- Following a healthy diet low in sugar and salt.
- Engaging in regular exercise.
- Adhering to a prescribed treatment plan, which may involve insulin or other medications.
- Maintaining a healthy weight.

Types of Kidney Disease:

Chronic kidney disease (CKD) occurs when the kidneys sustain long-term damage, leading to a decline in their capacity to effectively filter waste and fluid from the bloodstream. The accumulation of waste within the body can have detrimental effects on one's health. As time progresses, the damage to the kidneys and their functionality can deteriorate, eventually resulting in kidney failure or end-stage renal disease, wherein the kidneys cease to function entirely.

- **Fabry disease**: An uncommon hereditary condition characterised by the malfunctioning of various organs in the body, including the heart, brain, and kidneys. It hinders the adequate supply of blood to these organs, potentially resulting in chronic kidney disease or kidney failure.
- **Cystinosis**: A rare disorder where the accumulation of a natural chemical called cystine in the body causes health complications. Kidney damage caused by cystinosis can lead to kidney failure. Individuals with cystinosis must take medication to reduce their cystine levels and may require a kidney transplant. Cystinosis is inherited and is typically diagnosed in infancy.
- **Glomerulonephritis**: Refers to the impairment and loss of functionality in the tiny filters (glomeruli) within the kidneys responsible for purifying the blood. As a consequence, waste and fluid removal from the blood becomes compromised, potentially leading to kidney failure. Glomerulonephritis can arise from various health conditions, and treatment depends on the underlying cause.
- **IgA nephropathy**: A disease where proteins produced by the immune system accumulate in the kidneys, causing damage to the glomeruli, the blood-filtering units. The development of this damage is gradual, often unnoticed by individuals affected. Over time, IgA nephropathy can progress to chronic kidney disease, kidney failure, or even death. While there is no cure for IgA nephropathy, medications can slow down kidney damage.
- **Lupus nephritis**: An autoimmune disease characterised by inflammation, pain, and damage throughout the body, including the kidneys. This can result in chronic kidney disease or kidney failure. The exact cause of lupus nephritis is unknown, and it cannot be cured. However, with treatment, many people with lupus can manage symptoms and prevent severe kidney damage.
- **aHUS** (atypical hemolytic uremic syndrome): An exceedingly rare genetic disease that tends to run in families. It causes the formation of small blood clots within the body's small blood vessels. These clots can obstruct blood flow to the kidneys and other organs, leading to damage. Not all individuals with aHUS experience symptoms, but for those who do, symptoms often manifest after a triggering event, such as pregnancy or cancer.
- **Polycystic kidney disease (PKD)**: An inherited disorder that causes the growth of fluid-filled cysts on the kidneys and other organs. These cysts can diminish the kidney's capacity to filter waste and fluid from the blood. Over time, PKD can progress to kidney failure. While there is no cure for PKD, treatments can slow down cyst growth and mitigate associated health issues.
- **Other rare diseases**: Various other rare diseases can impair kidney function, reducing their ability to filter waste and fluid from the blood. This damage can result in chronic kidney disease or kidney failure.

Diet for Those Suffering from Nephropathy:
A proper diet plays a crucial role in managing nephropathy, a condition that affects kidney function. Here are some dietary recommendations for individuals suffering from nephropathy:

1. Limit protein intake: Since the kidneys may have difficulty processing and eliminating waste products from protein metabolism, it's recommended to limit the amount of protein in your diet. Consult a

healthcare professional or a registered dietitian to determine the appropriate protein intake for your specific condition.
2. Control sodium (salt) intake: Excessive sodium consumption can lead to fluid retention and high blood pressure, which can strain the kidneys. Limit your sodium intake by avoiding processed and packaged foods, restaurant meals, and adding salt to your meals. Instead, use herbs, spices, and other seasonings to enhance the flavour of your food.
3. Monitor potassium levels: Some individuals with nephropathy may have high levels of potassium in their blood, which can be harmful to the heart and other organs. Limit potassium-rich foods, such as bananas, oranges, tomatoes, potatoes, and avocado. Your healthcare provider or dietitian can guide you on maintaining a suitable potassium balance.
4. Manage phosphorus intake: Impaired kidney function can lead to high levels of phosphorus in the blood, causing bone and heart problems. Restrict phosphorus-rich foods like dairy products, nuts, seeds, chocolate, and fizzy drinks. Consider using phosphorus binders as prescribed by your healthcare provider to help control phosphorus levels.
5. Watch fluid intake: Depending on the severity of your kidney function, you may need to restrict fluid intake to avoid fluid overload. This is especially important if you experience swelling (oedema) or have difficulty breathing due to fluid retention. Your healthcare provider or dietitian can advise you on the appropriate fluid limits for your condition.
6. Monitor carbohydrates: If you have diabetes in addition to nephropathy, it's important to manage your blood sugar levels. Monitor your carbohydrate intake and follow any recommendations provided by your healthcare team to maintain stable blood sugar levels.
7. Individualise your diet: It's essential to work with a registered dietitian who specialises in renal nutrition. They can assess your specific needs, consider your medical history, medications, and lab results, and create a personalised meal plan that meets your nutritional requirements while managing nephropathy.

5 Simple Steps to Slow Down Nephropathy:

To slow down the progression of nephropathy (kidney damage), it's crucial to take proactive steps to maintain kidney health. Below are 5 simple steps you can follow:

1. Get your blood pressure under control: High blood pressure can worsen kidney damage. Follow a low-sodium diet, engage in regular physical activity, and take prescribed blood pressure medications as directed. Regularly monitor your blood pressure and strive to maintain a healthy range.
2. Manage your blood sugar levels: If you have diabetes, effectively controlling your blood sugar levels is vital. Monitor your blood glucose levels consistently, adhere to your prescribed diabetes management plan, take medications as instructed, and follow a balanced diet that promotes stable blood sugar levels. Keeping your blood sugar within the target range can help prevent or slow down kidney damage.
3. Maintain a healthy weight: Excess weight can strain the kidneys and contribute to the progression of nephropathy. Strive to achieve and sustain a healthy weight by combining regular physical activity with

a balanced, portion-controlled diet. Seek guidance from a healthcare professional or registered dietitian to develop a personalised weight management plan that suits your specific needs.
4. Embrace a kidney-friendly diet: Adopt a diet that supports kidney health. This typically involves reducing protein intake, limiting sodium consumption, managing phosphorus and potassium levels, and monitoring fluid intake, as described in the previous response on the diet for nephropathy. Collaborate with a registered dietitian specialising in renal nutrition to create a customised meal plan that suits your dietary requirements.
5. Stay hydrated and avoid kidney-damaging substances: Maintaining proper hydration is crucial for kidney function and overall well-being. Consult your healthcare provider to determine the appropriate fluid intake for your condition. Additionally, steer clear of substances that can harm the kidneys, such as excessive alcohol, certain medications, and toxins. Follow your healthcare provider's advice regarding medications and exercise caution when using over-the-counter drugs and herbal supplements.

Why Maintain an Adequate Water Balance?

Maintaining an adequate water balance is crucial for overall health and well-being due to several important reasons:

- Proper hydration: Water is essential to keep the body properly hydrated, supporting vital functions like digestion, circulation, temperature regulation, and nutrient absorption. It ensures the transport of nutrients and oxygen to cells, the elimination of waste products, and the lubrication of joints and tissues.
- Kidney function: The kidneys are responsible for maintaining water balance by filtering waste products and excess fluid from the blood, producing urine, and regulating electrolyte levels. Optimal kidney function depends on sufficient water intake, which promotes efficient filtration and prevents the formation of kidney stones by diluting urine.
- Fluid balance: Maintaining the right balance of fluids is critical for optimal body functioning. Throughout the day, the body loses water through activities like sweating, breathing, and urination. Regular water intake replenishes this lost fluid, preserving fluid balance and preventing dehydration and associated health issues such as electrolyte imbalances.
- Digestion and metabolism: Water is vital for digestion and metabolism. It aids in the breakdown of food, facilitates nutrient absorption, and supports the elimination of waste through bowel movements. Sufficient water intake promotes a healthy digestive system, prevents constipation, and supports overall gastrointestinal well-being.
- Physical performance and cognitive function: Proper hydration is essential for peak physical and mental performance. During physical activity, adequate water intake helps regulate body temperature, maintain adequate blood volume, and support muscle function. Dehydration can lead to reduced exercise performance, fatigue, and impaired cognitive function, affecting concentration, memory, and mental clarity.

- Skin health: Well-hydrated skin appears more youthful, elastic, and healthy. Water plays a vital role in maintaining skin moisture and promoting overall skin health and appearance. Inadequate water intake can contribute to dry skin, wrinkles, and various skin-related problems.

What to Eat at The Restaurant:

When dining out with nephropathy (kidney disease), it's crucial to make mindful choices that promote kidney health. Here are tips on selecting the right foods:

1. Go for low-sodium options: Sodium can worsen kidney damage and high blood pressure. Choose dishes labeled as low-sodium or inquire about low-salt alternatives. Avoid adding extra salt and steer clear of high-sodium foods like processed meats, canned soups, and fried items.
2. Opt for lean protein: Protein is important, but excessive intake can strain the kidneys. Choose lean protein sources like grilled chicken, fish, or legumes. Avoid high-fat meats, processed meats, and excessive cheese.
3. Incorporate fruits & vegetables: Fruits and vegetables are generally kidney-friendly, being low in sodium and rich in nutrients. Opt for fresh or steamed options without added salt or high-sodium sauces. Consider potassium restrictions if advised, and choose lower-potassium options when necessary.
4. Limit phosphorus-rich foods: If phosphorus intake needs to be managed, restrict foods high in phosphorus, such as dairy, nuts, seeds, and processed foods. Inquire about ingredients and preparation methods to make informed choices.
5. Mind portion sizes: Restaurant servings are often larger than recommended portions, leading to excessive calorie and nutrient intake. Share a meal or request a half portion. Balance your plate with appropriate amounts of protein, grains, and vegetables.
6. Exercise caution with sauces and dressings: Many sauces, dressings, and condiments contain high sodium, phosphorus, and potassium. Request dressings on the side or choose lower-sodium options. Explore alternatives like lemon juice, herbs, or vinegar for added flavour.
7. Stay hydrated: Hydrate with water or unsweetened beverages. Avoid sugary drinks, which can contribute to excessive calories and may not be suitable for certain kidney conditions.

Shopping List:

What to Eat:

A renal diet, also known as a kidney-friendly diet, aims to manage the intake of certain nutrients to support kidney function and minimise the risk of complications. Here are some recommended foods to include in a renal diet:

1. High-quality protein sources: Opt for lean proteins such as skinless poultry, fish, eggs, and plant-based protein sources like legumes and tofu. These provide essential amino acids while minimising the burden on the kidneys.
2. Low-potassium fruits and vegetables: Choose fruits and vegetables with lower potassium content, such as apples, berries, grapes, cabbage, cauliflower, green beans, and lettuce. Be cautious with high-potassium fruits like bananas, oranges, and kiwis, and high-potassium vegetables like tomatoes and potatoes.
3. Low-phosphorus foods: Limit phosphorus-rich foods and opt for lower-phosphorus alternatives. Examples include fresh fruits, vegetables, white bread, rice, and pasta. Dairy products, nuts, seeds, and processed foods tend to be higher in phosphorus and should be consumed in moderation.
4. Limited sodium: Reduce sodium intake by avoiding processed and packaged foods, canned soups, deli meats, and fast food. Instead, choose fresh or homemade meals and use herbs, spices, and other low-sodium seasonings to enhance flavours.
5. Controlled fluid intake: Depending on your specific needs, your healthcare provider may recommend monitoring your fluid intake. In general, it's important to stay hydrated but avoid excessive fluid consumption. Follow your healthcare provider's advice on fluid restrictions.
6. Healthy fats: Incorporate sources of healthy fats, such as avocados, olive oil, and fatty fish like salmon, which provide omega-3 fatty acids. Limit saturated and trans fats found in fried foods, fatty cuts of meat, and processed snacks.
7. Limited phosphorus additives: Be cautious of additives like phosphoric acid, which can be found in colas and some processed foods. These can contribute to higher phosphorus levels in the body.

What to Avoid:

On a renal diet, there are certain foods that are generally recommended to be avoided or limited due to their high content of certain nutrients that can potentially burden the kidneys. Here are some foods to avoid or restrict on a renal diet:

1. High-potassium foods: Limit or avoid high-potassium foods such as bananas, oranges, kiwis, potatoes, tomatoes, spinach, and avocados. These foods can raise potassium levels in the blood, which can be problematic for individuals with compromised kidney function.
2. High-phosphorus foods: Restrict foods rich in phosphorus, including dairy products (milk, cheese, yoghurt), nuts, seeds, legumes, whole grains, and processed foods. Excess phosphorus can lead to mineral imbalances and bone problems.
3. High-sodium foods: Minimise sodium intake by avoiding processed and packaged foods, canned soups, deli meats, fast food, and salty snacks. High sodium levels can contribute to fluid retention and increased blood pressure.
4. High-protein foods: While protein is important, excessive protein intake can put strain on the kidneys. Limit consumption of red meat, organ meats, high-fat meats, and processed meats. Moderation is key, and it's recommended to consult with a dietitian to determine the appropriate protein intake for your individual needs.

5. Fluids: Depending on your specific condition, you may need to monitor your fluid intake. Your healthcare provider will advise you on the appropriate amount of fluids to consume. It's important to balance hydration while avoiding excessive fluid retention.
6. Phosphorus additives: Watch out for phosphorus additives like phosphoric acid, often found in colas and some processed foods. These additives can contribute to elevated phosphorus levels.

Eating in England and Kidney Problems:

Traditional British food's got its charm, but if you're dealing with kidney problems, it's wise to tweak your choices. Here's how:
- Light brekkies: Skip the bacon and sausages. Go for low-sodium cereals, fruit, or a small portion of boiled eggs to kick-start the day.
- Simple lunches: When dining out, aim for low-sodium, low-phosphorus options. Avoid fried stuff, and stick to salads, sarnies with lean protein like chicken or fish, and light sides.
- Controlled afternoon tea: For afternoon tea, choose low-sugar, low-fat treats like wholemeal biscuits or fruit. Skip overly sugary scones and pastries.
- Balanced dinners: For dinner, opt for low-sodium, low-potassium, and low-phosphorus dishes. Go for lean meat or grilled fish, with veggie sides like carrots or green beans.

Chapter 1. Breakfast Recipes

COLD RECIPES

1. AVOCADO AND TOMATO RICE CAKES

-

Preparation Time: 5 minutes
Servings: 2

Ingredients:
- Rice cakes: 4
- Avocado: 1, mashed
- Cherry tomatoes: 8, halved
- Olive oil: 1 tsp
- Black pepper: 1/4 tsp

Directions:
Introduction: A light and healthy breakfast option. Spread the mashed avocado on each rice cake. Top with cherry tomatoes and drizzle with olive oil. Sprinkle with black pepper.

Nutritional Information (per serving):
Calories: 140 kcal, Fat: 7g (0.25 oz), Carbs: 18g (0.64 oz), Protein: 3g (0.11 oz), Sodium: 50mg, Potassio: 160mg, Fosforo: 70mg

Storage: Best eaten fresh.

Presentation: Serve on a plate, garnished with fresh basil leaves.

Variation: Use cucumber slices instead of cherry tomatoes for a different twist.

2. COTTAGE CHEESE AND BERRY BOWL

Preparation Time: 5 minutes
Servings: 2

Ingredients:
- Cottage cheese: 1 cup
- Strawberries: 1/2 cup, hulled and sliced
- Blueberries: 1/2 cup
- Honey: 1 tbsp

Directions:
Introduction: A protein-rich, low-fat breakfast. Mix cottage cheese with honey. Divide into bowls. Top with strawberries and blueberries.

Nutritional Information (per serving):
Calories: 180 kcal, Fat: 4g (0.14 oz), Carbs: 20g (0.71 oz), Protein: 15g (0.53 oz), Sodium: 120mg, Potassio: 200mg, Fosforo: 130mg

Storage: Best eaten fresh.

Presentation: Serve in bowls, with a mint sprig garnish.

Variation: Add a sprinkle of chia seeds for extra fiber.

3. FRUIT SALAD

Preparation Time: 10 minutes
Cooking Time: 0 minutes
Servings: 4

Ingredients:
- Strawberries: 1 cup (150g / 5.29 oz)

- Blueberries: 1 cup (150g / 5.29 oz)
- Grapes: 1 cup (150g / 5.29 oz)
- Mint: 1 tbsp (5g / 0.18 oz)

Directions:
Introduction: A refreshing, light breakfast or snack.
Preparation: Chop the strawberries and mix with blueberries, grapes, and mint.

Nutritional Information (per serving):
Calories: 80 kcal, Fat: 0g, Carbs: 20g (0.7 oz), Protein: 1g (0.04 oz), Sodium: 5mg, Potassium: 100mg, Phosphorus: 20mg

Storage: Best eaten fresh.

Presentation: Serve in bowls with a garnish of mint leaves.

Variations: Add a drizzle of low-sugar yogurt for extra creaminess.

4. GREEK YOGURT AND HONEY PARFAIT

Preparation Time: 5 minutes
Servings: 2

Ingredients:
- Greek yogurt: 1 cup
- Honey: 2 tbsp
- Granola: 1/4 cup
- Blueberries: 1/2 cup

Directions:
Introduction: A simple and nutritious parfait for a balanced breakfast.
Layer Greek yogurt, honey, granola, and blueberries in a glass. Repeat layers until ingredients are used up.

Nutritional Information (per serving):
Calories: 250 kcal, Fat: 8g (0.28 oz), Carbs: 38g (1.34 oz), Protein: 10g (0.35 oz), Sodium: 75mg, Potassio: 180mg, Fosforo: 120mg

Storage: Best eaten fresh.

Presentation: Serve in a clear glass to showcase the layers.

Variation: Substitute strawberries for blueberries.

5. MARMALADE AND TOAST

Preparation Time: 5 minutes
Cooking Time: 5 minutes
Servings: 4

Ingredients:
- Wholemeal bread: 4 slices
- Butter: 2 tbsp (30g / 1 oz)
- Marmalade: 1/4 cup (60g / 2.11 oz)

Directions:
Introduction: A classic breakfast option, pairing toast with marmalade.
Preparation: Toast the bread slices. Spread with butter, then marmalade.

Nutritional Information (per serving):
Calories: 150 kcal, Fat: 6g (0.21 oz), Carbs: 25g (0.88 oz), Protein: 3g (0.1 oz), Sodium: 100mg, Potassium: 80mg, Phosphorus: 50mg

Storage: Best eaten fresh.

Presentation: Serve with a cup of tea.

Variations: Replace butter with a plant-based spread for lactose-intolerant individuals.

6. SCONE AND BUTTER

Preparation Time: 10 minutes
Cooking Time: 12 minutes
Servings: 4

Ingredients:

- Flour: 2 cups (240g / 8.47 oz)
- Butter: 1/2 cup (110g / 3.88 oz)
- Baking powder: 2 tsp (10g / 0.35 oz)
- Milk: 1/2 cup (120ml / 4 oz)
- Salt: a pinch

Directions:

Introduction: A simple, classic British breakfast or afternoon tea option.
Preparation: Mix flour, butter, and baking powder. Add milk until dough forms. Roll out and cut into rounds.
Cooking: Bake in an oven at 400°F (200°C) for 12 minutes.

Nutritional Information (per serving):
Calories: 200 kcal, Fat: 10g (0.35 oz), Carbs: 25g (0.88 oz), Protein: 4g (0.14 oz), Sodium: 150mg, Potassium: 100mg, Phosphorus: 80mg

Storage: Can be stored in an airtight container for up to two days.
Presentation: Serve with butter and a low-sugar jam.
Variations: Substitute regular flour with gluten-free flour for those with gluten intolerance.

7. SIMPLE FRUIT PARFAIT

Preparation Time: 5 minutes
Cooking Time: 0 minutes
Servings: 4

Ingredients:

- Low-fat yogurt: 2 cups (500g / 17.6 oz)
- Mixed berries: 1 cup (150g / 5.29 oz)
- Low-sugar granola: 1/2 cup (60g / 2.11 oz)

Directions:
Introduction: A light, layered dish perfect for a refreshing breakfast.
Assemblage: Layer yogurt, berries, and granola in a clear glass or bowl.

Nutritional Information (per serving):
Calories: 180 kcal, Fat: 4g (0.14 oz), Carbs: 25g (0.88 oz), Protein: 8g (0.28 oz), Sodium: 100mg, Potassium: 120mg, Phosphorus: 60mg

Storage: Best eaten fresh.
Presentation: Serve in a glass, with a mint garnish.
Variations: Use a plant-based yogurt for a dairy-free option.

8. TEACAKE AND JAM

Preparation Time: 5 minutes
Cooking Time: 5 minutes
Servings: 4

Ingredients:

- Teacakes: 4
- Butter: 2 tbsp (30g / 1 oz)
- Low-sugar jam: 1/4 cup (60g / 2.11 oz)

Directions:
Introduction: A traditional sweet breakfast or snack, great with tea.
Preparation: Toast each teacake, spread with butter, and add jam.

Nutritional Information (per serving):
Calories: 180 kcal, Fat: 8g (0.28 oz), Carbs: 25g (0.88 oz), Protein: 4g (0.14 oz), Sodium: 100mg, Potassium: 60mg, Phosphorus: 40mg

Storage: Best eaten fresh.

Presentation: Serve with a cup of tea.

Variations: Replace the butter with a dairy-free spread for lactose-intolerant individuals.

9. WHOLEMEAL TOAST WITH MARMITE

Preparation Time: 5 minutes
Cooking Time: 5 minutes
Servings: 4

Ingredients:
- Wholemeal bread: 4 slices
- Butter: 2 tbsp (30g / 1 oz)
- Marmite: 2 tbsp

Directions:
Introduction: A quintessential British breakfast with a savory twist.
Preparation: Toast the bread slices. Spread each slice with butter, then add a thin layer of Marmite.

Nutritional Information (per serving):
Calories: 100 kcal, Fat: 4g (0.14 oz), Carbs: 15g (0.53 oz), Protein: 5g (0.18 oz), Sodium: 200mg, Potassium: 60mg, Phosphorus: 50mg

Storage: Best eaten fresh.
Presentation: Serve with a cup of tea or coffee.
Variations: For a dairy-free option, replace butter with a plant-based spread.

10. YOGURT AND GRANOLA

Preparation Time: 5 minutes
Cooking Time: 0 minutes
Servings: 4

Ingredients:
- Low-fat yogurt: 2 cups (500g / 17.6 oz)
- Low-sugar granola: 1 cup (120g / 4.23 oz)
- Berries: 1 cup (150g / 5.29 oz)

Directions:
Introduction: A light, healthy breakfast option with a variety of textures.
Assemblage: Layer yogurt, granola, and berries in a bowl.

Nutritional Information (per serving):
Calories: 200 kcal, Fat: 5g (0.18 oz), Carbs: 30g (1.05 oz), Protein: 10g (0.35 oz), Sodium: 100mg, Potassium: 150mg, Phosphorus: 80mg

Storage: Best eaten fresh.
Presentation: Serve in bowls, garnished with extra berries.
Variations: For a dairy-free option, use plant-based yogurt.

Certamente! Ecco tre ricette fredde per la colazione inglese che non richiedono cottura:

HOT RECIPES

11. AVOCADO TOAST

Preparation Time: 5 minutes
Cooking Time: 5 minutes
Servings: 4

Ingredients:
- Wholemeal bread: 4 slices
- Avocado: 1 large
- Lemon juice: 1 tbsp (15ml / 0.53 oz)

- Salt: a pinch
- Black pepper: a pinch

Directions:
Introduction: A modern, healthy twist to start the day.
Preparation: Mash the avocado with lemon juice, salt, and pepper. Toast the bread slices.
Assemblage: Spread the avocado mixture on each slice.

Nutritional Information (per serving):
Calories: 150 kcal, Fat: 10g (0.35 oz), Carbs: 15g (0.53 oz), Protein: 4g (0.14 oz), Sodium: 150mg, Potassium: 180mg, Phosphorus: 80mg

Storage: Best eaten fresh.
Presentation: Serve with a sprinkle of chili flakes for extra flavor.
Variations: For a gluten-free option, use gluten-free bread.

12. BANANA PANCAKES

Preparation Time: 10 minutes
Cooking Time: 10 minutes
Servings: 4

Ingredients:
- Flour: 1 cup (120g / 4.23 oz)
- Milk: 1/2 cup (120ml / 4 oz)
- Egg: 1 large
- Banana: 1, mashed
- Baking powder: 1 tsp (5g / 0.18 oz)
- Butter: 2 tbsp (30g / 1 oz)

Directions:
Introduction: A sweet and satisfying breakfast option, combining pancakes and banana.
Preparation: Mix flour, baking powder, milk, egg, and banana until smooth.
Cooking: Heat butter in a pan, pouring in batter in spoonfuls. Cook until bubbles form, then flip and cook until golden brown.

Nutritional Information (per serving):
Calories: 200 kcal, Fat: 8g (0.28 oz), Carbs: 30g (1.05 oz), Protein: 6g (0.21 oz), Sodium: 150mg, Potassium: 150mg, Phosphorus: 80mg

Storage: Best eaten fresh.
Presentation: Serve with a drizzle of honey or maple syrup.
Variations: Substitute flour with gluten-free flour for gluten-intolerant individuals.

13. BEAN AND CHEESE TOASTIE

Preparation Time: 10 minutes
Cooking Time: 10 minutes
Servings: 4

Ingredients:
- Wholemeal bread: 8 slices
- Low-sodium baked beans: 1 can (415g / 14.6 oz)
- Low-fat cheese: 1 cup (120g / 4 oz)
- Butter: 2 tbsp (30g / 1 oz)

Directions:
Introduction: A warm and comforting dish that's both filling and satisfying.
Assemblage: Spread butter on the bread slices. Layer baked beans and cheese between two slices.
Cooking: Toast in a sandwich press until golden brown.

Nutritional Information (per serving):

Calories: 300 kcal, Fat: 12g (0.42 oz), Carbs: 40g (1.41 oz), Protein: 15g (0.53 oz), Sodium: 350mg, Potassium: 200mg, Phosphorus: 150mg

Storage: Best eaten fresh.

Presentation: Serve with a side of mixed greens.

Variations: Replace cheese with a dairy-free alternative for lactose-intolerant individuals.

14. BRAN MUFFINS

Preparation Time: 10 minutes
Cooking Time: 20 minutes
Servings: 4

Ingredients:
- Bran flakes: 1 cup (50g / 1.76 oz)
- Flour: 1 cup (120g / 4.23 oz)
- Baking powder: 1 tsp (5g / 0.18 oz)
- Sugar: 1/4 cup (60g / 2.11 oz)
- Milk: 1/2 cup (120ml / 4 oz)
- Egg: 1 large
- Butter: 1/4 cup (60g / 2.11 oz)

Directions:
Introduction: A wholesome breakfast muffin, combining bran flakes for fibre with a touch of sweetness.
Preparation: Mix bran flakes, flour, baking powder, and sugar. Add milk, egg, and melted butter, stirring until smooth.
Cooking: Divide into a muffin tin and bake at 375°F (190°C) for 15-20 minutes.

Nutritional Information (per serving):
Calories: 150 kcal, Fat: 7g (0.25 oz), Carbs: 20g (0.7 oz), Protein: 4g (0.14 oz), Sodium: 150mg, Potassium: 80mg, Phosphorus: 60mg

Storage: Can be stored in an airtight container for up to 3 days.

Presentation: Serve warm or at room temperature.

Variations: Substitute butter with a plant-based alternative for a vegan option.

15. CHEESE AND TOMATO TOASTIE

Preparation Time: 5 minutes
Cooking Time: 10 minutes
Servings: 4

Ingredients:
- Wholemeal bread: 8 slices
- Low-fat cheese: 1 cup (120g / 4 oz)
- Tomato, sliced: 1 large
- Butter: 2 tbsp (30g / 1 oz)

Directions:
Introduction: A warm, satisfying dish, pairing cheese and tomatoes for a classic toastie.
Assemblage: Spread butter on the bread slices. Layer cheese and tomato slices between two slices.
Cooking: Toast in a sandwich press until golden brown.

Nutritional Information (per serving):
Calories: 250 kcal, Fat: 10g (0.35 oz), Carbs: 30g (1.05 oz), Protein: 12g (0.42 oz), Sodium: 200mg, Potassium: 150mg, Phosphorus: 120mg

Storage: Best eaten fresh.

Presentation: Serve with a side salad or fruit.

Variations: Replace cheese with a dairy-free alternative for lactose-intolerant individuals.

16. CINNAMON TOAST

Preparation Time: 5 minutes
Cooking Time: 5 minutes
Servings: 4

Ingredients:
- Wholemeal bread: 4 slices
- Butter: 2 tbsp (30g / 1 oz)
- Sugar: 1 tbsp (15g / 0.53 oz)
- Cinnamon: 1/2 tsp

Directions:
Introduction: A sweet and simple breakfast option, perfect for starting the day.
Preparation: Toast the bread slices. Mix sugar and cinnamon together.
Assemblage: Spread butter on each slice, followed by a sprinkle of cinnamon sugar.

Nutritional Information (per serving):
Calories: 120 kcal, Fat: 5g (0.18 oz), Carbs: 20g (0.7 oz), Protein: 3g (0.1 oz), Sodium: 100mg, Potassium: 60mg, Phosphorus: 50mg

Storage: Best eaten fresh.

Presentation: Serve with a cup of tea or coffee.

Variations: For a dairy-free option, replace butter with a plant-based spread.

17. CRUMPETS AND JAM

Preparation Time: 5 minutes
Cooking Time: 5 minutes
Servings: 4

Ingredients:
- Crumpets: 4
- Butter: 2 tbsp (30g / 1 oz)
- Low-sugar jam: 1/4 cup (60g / 2 oz)

Directions:
Introduction: A classic British breakfast or tea-time treat.
Preparation: Toast each crumpet until golden brown. Spread with butter and jam.

Nutritional Information (per serving):
Calories: 160 kcal, Fat: 6g (0.21 oz), Carbs: 25g (0.88 oz), Protein: 4g (0.14 oz), Sodium: 150mg, Potassium: 80mg, Phosphorus: 50mg

Storage: Best eaten fresh.

Presentation: Serve with a cup of tea.

Variations: Replace butter with a dairy-free spread for those with lactose intolerance.

18. EGG AND SPINACH WRAP

Preparation Time: 5 minutes
Cooking Time: 10 minutes
Servings: 4

Ingredients:
- Eggs: 4 large
- Milk: 1/4 cup (60ml / 2 oz)
- Spinach: 1 cup (50g / 1.76 oz)
- Whole wheat wraps: 4
- Salt: a pinch
- Black pepper: a pinch

Directions:
Introduction: A nutritious wrap, combining eggs and spinach for a balanced breakfast.
Preparation: Beat the eggs with milk, salt, and pepper.
Cooking: Cook the spinach until wilted, then add the egg mixture, stirring until scrambled.
Assemblage: Fill each wrap with the egg-spinach mixture, folding into a burrito shape.

Nutritional Information (per serving):
Calories: 200 kcal, Fat: 10g (0.35 oz), Carbs: 15g (0.53 oz), Protein: 15g (0.53 oz), Sodium: 150mg, Potassium: 150mg, Phosphorus: 120mg

Storage: Best eaten fresh.

Presentation: Serve with a side of cherry tomatoes.

Variations: Use a dairy-free milk alternative for lactose-intolerant individuals.

19. EGGS BENEDICT

Preparation Time: 10 minutes
Cooking Time: 10 minutes
Servings: 4

Ingredients:
- *English muffins:* 2, halved
- *Butter:* 2 tbsp (30g / 1 oz)
- *Ham:* 4 slices
- *Eggs:* 4
- *Low-sodium Hollandaise sauce:* 1/2 cup (120ml / 4 oz)

Directions:
Introduction: A sophisticated breakfast dish featuring poached eggs on toasted muffins.
Preparation: Toast the muffins with butter. In a pot, bring water to a simmer, crack each egg into it, and poach until whites are set.
Assemblage: Place ham on each muffin half, followed by an egg. Drizzle with Hollandaise sauce.

Nutritional Information (per serving):
Calories: 280 kcal, Fat: 15g (0.53 oz), Carbs: 20g (0.7 oz), Protein: 20g (0.7 oz), Sodium: 550mg, Potassium: 250mg, Phosphorus: 220mg

Storage: This dish is best eaten fresh.

Presentation: Serve two halves on each plate, with the sauce generously drizzled on top.

Variations: Replace the ham with turkey slices or a vegetarian alternative to reduce sodium content.

20. ENGLISH MUFFIN WITH COTTAGE CHEESE AND CUCUMBER

Preparation Time: 5 minutes
Cooking Time: 0 minutes
Servings: 4

Ingredients:
- English muffins: 2, halved
- Cottage cheese: 1 cup (240g / 8 oz)
- Cucumber, sliced: 1/2 cup (120g / 4.2 oz)
- Dill: 1 tsp

Directions:
Introduction: A light, balanced breakfast option with a refreshing twist.
Assemblage: Toast the muffins and spread cottage cheese evenly on each half. Top with cucumber slices and a sprinkle of dill.

Nutritional Information (per serving):
Calories: 150 kcal, Fat: 5g (0.18 oz), Carbs: 20g (0.7 oz), Protein: 10g (0.35 oz), Sodium: 180mg, Potassium: 100mg, Phosphorus: 80mg

Storage: Best eaten fresh.

Presentation: Serve with a cup of tea or a light beverage.

Variations: Use ricotta cheese or a dairy-free spread for lactose-intolerant individuals.

21. FULL ENGLISH BREAKFAST

Preparation Time: 10 minutes
Cooking Time: 20 minutes
Servings: 4

Ingredients:
- Bacon: 4 slices
- Chicken sausages: 4
- Eggs: 4 large
- Mushrooms, sliced: 200g (7 oz)
- Cherry tomatoes: 1 cup (150g / 5.29 oz)
- Low-sodium baked beans: 1 can (415g / 14.6 oz)
- Wholemeal bread: 4 slices

Directions:
Introduction: A traditional Full English Breakfast is a hearty way to start the day, featuring a balanced combination of proteins and vegetables.
Preparation of Ingredients: Fry the bacon and sausages in a large skillet over medium heat until crispy. In another pan, sauté the mushrooms and tomatoes until tender.
Assemblage: Fry the eggs in a separate pan until the whites are set, or scramble them for a softer texture. Toast the bread slices.
Cooking: Cook the baked beans separately in a pot until heated through.
Serving: Plate all components together, balancing protein, vegetables, and carbohydrates.

Nutritional Information (per serving):
Calories: 450 kcal, Fat: 20g (0.7 oz), Carbs: 40g (1.41 oz), Protein: 25g (0.88 oz), Sodium: 700mg, Potassium: 400mg, Phosphorus: 300mg

Storage: This dish is best eaten fresh. Leftovers can be stored in an airtight container in the refrigerator for up to one day.

Presentation: Serve on a large plate, arranging the bacon, sausages, eggs, and bread evenly, with the mushrooms, tomatoes, and beans filling in the gaps.
Variations: Consider replacing the bacon with turkey rashers for a lower-fat option. Swap baked beans for low-potassium beans such as cannellini beans to reduce potassium content.

22. GRILLED TOMATOES AND MUSHROOMS

Preparation Time: 5 minutes
Cooking Time: 10 minutes
Servings: 4

Ingredients:
- Tomatoes: 4 large, halved
- Mushrooms, sliced: 200g (7 oz)
- Olive oil: 2 tbsp (30ml / 1 oz)
- Black pepper: 1/4 tsp
- Salt: a pinch

Directions:
Introduction: A simple and light breakfast dish, combining grilled tomatoes and sautéed mushrooms.
Cooking: Heat olive oil in a pan over medium heat, sautéing the mushrooms until golden. Grill tomatoes cut-side down until tender.
Serving: Plate the tomatoes and mushrooms together, seasoning with salt and pepper.

Nutritional Information (per serving):
Calories: 80 kcal, Fat: 4g (0.14 oz), Carbs: 10g (0.35 oz), Protein: 3g (0.1 oz), Sodium: 50mg, Potassium: 180mg, Phosphorus: 50mg

Storage: Best eaten fresh.
Presentation: Serve on a plate, garnished with fresh herbs.

Variations: Add garlic or herbs to the mushrooms for extra flavour.

23. PORRIDGE

Preparation Time: 5 minutes
Cooking Time: 10 minutes
Servings: 4

Ingredients:
- Oats: 1 cup (100g / 3.5 oz)
- Water: 2 cups (480ml / 16.9 oz)
- Milk: 1 cup (240ml / 8 oz)
- Salt: a pinch
- Honey: 2 tbsp (30ml / 1 oz)

Directions:
Introduction: A classic, creamy British breakfast that's warm and filling.
Preparation: In a pot, bring the water to a boil, then add the oats and salt. Cook until thickened, stirring frequently. Stir in the milk and continue cooking until absorbed.
Serving: Serve hot, drizzled with honey.

Nutritional Information (per serving):
Calories: 180 kcal, Fat: 3g (0.11 oz), Carbs: 30g (1.05 oz), Protein: 7g (0.25 oz), Sodium: 100mg, Potassium: 150mg, Phosphorus: 80mg

Storage: Leftovers can be refrigerated in an airtight container for up to two days. Reheat gently in a pot or microwave, adding milk or water if needed.

Presentation: Serve in a bowl, with the honey drizzled on top.

Variations: Swap the honey for a sugar substitute to reduce sugars or add fruits like berries for extra flavor.

24. RICE PUDDING

Preparation Time: 10 minutes
Cooking Time: 20 minutes
Servings: 4

Ingredients:
- Rice: 1 cup (180g / 6.35 oz)
- Water: 2 cups (480ml / 16.9 oz)
- Milk: 2 cups (480ml / 16.9 oz)
- Sugar: 1/4 cup (60g / 2.11 oz)
- Cinnamon: 1 tsp

Directions:
Introduction: A comforting, sweet breakfast or dessert dish.
Cooking: In a pot, cook rice with water until absorbed. Add milk and sugar, cooking until thickened.
Serving: Serve warm, with a sprinkle of cinnamon.

Nutritional Information (per serving):
Calories: 250 kcal, Fat: 4g (0.14 oz), Carbs: 45g (1.58 oz), Protein: 6g (0.21 oz), Sodium: 100mg, Potassium: 150mg, Phosphorus: 80mg

Storage: Can be refrigerated for up to two days.

Presentation: Serve in bowls, with a dusting of cinnamon.

Variations: Replace milk with almond or oat milk for a dairy-free option.

25. SCRAMBLED EGGS AND TOAST

Preparation Time: 5 minutes
Cooking Time: 5 minutes
Servings: 4

Ingredients:

- Eggs: 4 large
- Milk: 1/4 cup (60ml / 2 oz)
- Salt: a pinch
- Black pepper: a pinch
- Butter: 1 tbsp (15g / 0.53 oz)
- Wholemeal bread: 4 slices

Directions:

Introduction: A simple, classic breakfast option.
Preparation: Beat the eggs with milk, salt, and pepper.
Cooking: Melt butter in a pan, add the egg mixture, and scramble until just set. Toast the bread slices.

Nutritional Information (per serving):
Calories: 180 kcal, Fat: 10g (0.35 oz), Carbs: 10g (0.35 oz), Protein: 12g (0.42 oz), Sodium: 200mg, Potassium: 100mg, Phosphorus: 80mg

Storage: Best eaten fresh.

Presentation: Serve on a plate, with the scrambled eggs on top of the toast.

Variations: Add chopped chives or parsley for extra flavor

26. SMOKED HADDOCK AND POACHED EGG

Preparation Time: 10 minutes
Cooking Time: 15 minutes
Servings: 4

Ingredients:
- Smoked haddock fillets: 4
- Water: 4 cups (960ml / 32 oz)
- Vinegar: 1 tbsp (15ml / 0.53 oz)
- Eggs: 4 large
- Black pepper: 1/4 tsp

Directions:

Introduction: A classic British breakfast dish combining poached haddock and eggs.
Cooking: Simmer haddock in water until cooked through, about 10 minutes. In another pot, bring water with vinegar to a simmer, poaching each egg until whites are set.
Serving: Place haddock on a plate, topped with an egg and a dash of black pepper.

Nutritional Information (per serving):
Calories: 180 kcal, Fat: 5g (0.18 oz), Carbs: 2g (0.07 oz), Protein: 30g (1.05 oz), Sodium: 250mg, Potassium: 200mg, Phosphorus: 200mg

Storage: Best eaten fresh.

Presentation: Serve with a slice of wholemeal bread.

Variations: Swap haddock for cod for a milder flavour.

27. SMOKED SALMON AND CREAM CHEESE BAGEL

Preparation Time: 5 minutes
Cooking Time: 0 minutes
Servings: 4

Ingredients:
- Bagels: 4
- Low-fat cream cheese: 1/2 cup (120g / 4.23 oz)
- Smoked salmon: 200g (7 oz)
- Capers: 1 tbsp (15g / 0.53 oz)
- Dill: 1 tbsp

Directions:

Introduction: A modern take on a classic breakfast, combining smoked salmon with creamy cheese.
Preparation: Spread cream cheese on each bagel half, top with salmon, capers, and dill.

Nutritional Information (per serving):
Calories: 250 kcal, Fat: 10g (0.35 oz), Carbs: 30g (1.05 oz), Protein: 15g (0.53 oz), Sodium: 500mg, Potassium: 150mg, Phosphorus: 150mg

Storage: Best eaten fresh.

Presentation: Serve with a garnish of dill and lemon wedges.

Variations: Swap the cream cheese for a low-lactose version for lactose-intolerant individuals.

28. TOAST AND BAKED BEANS

Preparation Time: 5 minutes
Cooking Time: 5 minutes
Servings: 4

Ingredients:
- Wholemeal bread: 4 slices
- Low-sodium baked beans: 1 can (415g / 14.6 oz)
- Butter: 1 tbsp (15g / 0.53 oz)

Directions:
Introduction: A simple, classic British breakfast, pairing toast with baked beans.
Preparation: Toast the bread slices. Heat the baked beans in a pot until warm.
Assemblage: Spread butter on the toast and top with beans.

Nutritional Information (per serving):
Calories: 200 kcal, Fat: 5g (0.18 oz), Carbs: 35g (1.23 oz), Protein: 7g (0.25 oz), Sodium: 250mg, Potassium: 180mg, Phosphorus: 80mg

Storage: Best eaten fresh.

Presentation: Serve with a side of sliced tomatoes or cucumbers.

Variations: Replace butter with a dairy-free spread for lactose-intolerant individuals.

29. TOAST WITH EGG AND ASPARAGUS

Preparation Time: 5 minutes
Cooking Time: 10 minutes
Servings: 4

Ingredients:
- Wholemeal bread: 4 slices
- Eggs: 4 large
- Asparagus spears: 8
- Olive oil: 1 tbsp (15ml / 0.53 oz)
- Black pepper: 1/4 tsp

Directions:
Introduction: A balanced breakfast dish, combining protein, fibre, and vitamins.
Cooking: Grill the asparagus until tender. Fry or poach the eggs until whites are set. Toast the bread slices.
Assemblage: Top each slice of bread with 2 asparagus spears and an egg. Season with black pepper.

Nutritional Information (per serving):
Calories: 160 kcal, Fat: 8g (0.28 oz), Carbs: 10g (0.35 oz), Protein: 12g (0.42 oz), Sodium: 120mg, Potassium: 150mg, Phosphorus: 100mg

Storage: Best eaten fresh.

Presentation: Serve on a plate, with a side of mixed greens.

Variations: For a vegan option, skip the egg and use tofu.

30. VEGETABLE BREAKFAST HASH

Preparation Time: 10 minutes
Cooking Time: 15 minutes
Servings: 4

Ingredients:
- Potatoes, diced: 1 cup (150g / 5.29 oz)
- Olive oil: 2 tbsp (30ml / 1 oz)
- Onion, chopped: 1 medium
- Red bell pepper, diced: 1
- Courgette, diced: 1
- Eggs: 4 large
- Black pepper: 1/4 tsp

Directions:
Introduction: A hearty breakfast hash, perfect for those seeking a balanced, vegetable-packed dish.
Preparation: Heat oil in a large skillet over medium heat. Add potatoes and cook until golden, about 10 minutes.
Cooking: Add onion, bell pepper, and courgette, cooking until tender. In a separate pan, fry or scramble the eggs, seasoning with black pepper.
Assemblage: Serve the hash topped with an egg.

Nutritional Information (per serving):
Calories: 250 kcal, Fat: 12g (0.42 oz), Carbs: 20g (0.7 oz), Protein: 12g (0.42 oz), Sodium: 200mg, Potassium: 250mg, Phosphorus: 150mg

Storage: Best eaten fresh.
Presentation: Serve on a plate, garnished with fresh herbs.
Variations: Swap the potatoes for sweet potatoes to lower potassium, or skip the egg for a vegan option.

31. VEGGIE OMELETTE

Preparation Time: 10 minutes
Cooking Time: 10 minutes
Servings: 4

Ingredients:
- Eggs: 4 large
- Milk: 1/4 cup (60ml / 2 oz)
- Low-fat cheese: 1/4 cup (30g / 1 oz)
- Spinach: 1 cup (50g / 1.76 oz)
- Mushrooms: 1 cup (100g / 3.52 oz)
- Butter: 1 tbsp (15g / 0.53 oz)

Directions:
Introduction: A nutritious start to the day, packed with vegetables.
Preparation: Beat the eggs with milk. In a skillet, sauté mushrooms and spinach until tender.
Assemblage: Add egg mixture and cheese, cooking until set.

Nutritional Information (per serving):
Calories: 200 kcal, Fat: 10g (0.35 oz), Carbs: 5g (0.18 oz), Protein: 18g (0.63 oz), Sodium: 300mg, Potassium: 200mg, Phosphorus: 150mg

Storage: Best eaten fresh.
Presentation: Serve on a plate with a side of wholemeal toast.
Variations: For a dairy-free option, skip the cheese or use a vegan cheese alternative.

32. WHOLEMEAL MUFFINS

Preparation Time: 10 minutes
Cooking Time: 20 minutes
Servings: 4

Ingredients:

- Wholemeal flour: 1 cup (120g / 4.23 oz)
- Baking powder: 1 tsp (5g / 0.18 oz)
- Milk: 1/2 cup (120ml / 4 oz)
- Egg: 1 large
- Sugar: 1/4 cup (60g / 2.11 oz)
- Olive oil: 1/4 cup (60ml / 2.11 oz)

Directions:

Introduction: A wholesome, fibre-rich muffin, great for a healthy breakfast.

Preparation: Mix flour, baking powder, and sugar. Add milk, egg, and olive oil, stirring until smooth.

Cooking: Divide into a muffin tin and bake at 375°F (190°C) for 15-20 minutes.

Nutritional Information (per serving):
Calories: 160 kcal, Fat: 7g (0.25 oz), Carbs: 20g (0.7 oz), Protein: 4g (0.14 oz), Sodium: 150mg, Potassium: 80mg, Phosphorus: 60mg

Storage: Can be stored in an airtight container for up to 3 days.

Presentation: Serve warm or at room temperature.

Variations: Add dried fruit or nuts for extra texture.

SMOOTHIES

33. APPLE AND OAT SMOOTHIE

Preparation Time: 5 minutes
Servings: 2

Ingredients:
- Apple juice: 1 cup
- Rolled oats: 1/4 cup
- Greek yogurt: 1/2 cup
- Honey: 1 tbsp
- Ice cubes

Directions:

Introduction: A balanced blend of fruits and grains. Blend all ingredients until smooth. Serve chilled.

Nutritional Information (per serving):
Calories: 150 kcal, Fat: 4g (0.14 oz), Carbs: 22g (0.77 oz), Protein: 5g (0.18 oz), Sodium: 45mg, Potassium: 180mg, Phosphorus: 70mg

Presentation: Serve in a tall glass with a sprinkle of cinnamon on top. Garnish with an apple slice.

Variation: Substitute almond milk for Greek yogurt for a dairy-free option.

34. BERRY BLAST SMOOTHIE

Preparation Time: 5 minutes
Servings: 2

Ingredients:
- Blueberries: 1/2 cup
- Raspberries: 1/2 cup
- Greek yogurt: 1 cup
- Almond milk: 1/2 cup
- Honey: 1 tsp
- Ice cubes

Directions:

Introduction: A fruity blend, rich in vitamins and antioxidants.
Blend all ingredients until smooth. Serve immediately.

Nutritional Information (per serving):
Calories: 160 kcal, Fat: 3g (0.11 oz), Carbs: 30g (1.06 oz), Protein: 8g (0.28 oz), Sodium: 35mg, Potassium: 220mg, Phosphorus: 80mg

Presentation: Serve in a chilled glass with a berry garnish on top. Optionally, add a small umbrella.

Variation: Substitute soy milk for almond milk for a nut-free option.

35. BLUEBERRY-BANANA SMOOTHIE

Preparation Time: 5 minutes
Servings: 2

Ingredients:
- Blueberries: 1 cup
- Banana: 1, peeled
- Greek yogurt: 1 cup
- Almond milk: 1 cup
- Honey: 1 tbsp
- Ice cubes

Directions:
Introduction: A creamy and nutritious smoothie, rich in antioxidants.
Blend all ingredients until smooth. Serve immediately.

Nutritional Information (per serving):
Calories: 160 kcal, Fat: 3g (0.11 oz), Carbs: 30g (1.06 oz), Protein: 7g (0.25 oz), Sodium: 35mg, Potassium: 200mg, Phosphorus: 80mg

Presentation: Serve in a clear glass with a blueberry garnish on top.

Variation: Substitute soy milk for almond milk for a nut-free option.

36. CARROT-ORANGE SMOOTHIE

Preparation Time: 5 minutes
Servings: 2

Ingredients:
- Carrot juice: 1 cup
- Orange juice: 1 cup
- Greek yogurt: 1/2 cup
- Honey: 1 tbsp
- Ice cubes

Directions:
Introduction: A vibrant and nutritious smoothie, rich in vitamins A and C.
Blend all ingredients until smooth. Serve chilled.

Nutritional Information (per serving):
Calories: 160 kcal, Fat: 3g (0.11 oz), Carbs: 28g (0.99 oz), Protein: 5g (0.18 oz), Sodium: 35mg, Potassium: 150mg, Phosphorus: 60mg

Presentation: Serve in a clear glass with an orange wedge on the rim.

Variation: Add a teaspoon of ginger for extra warmth.

37. CUCUMBER-MINT REFRESHER

Preparation Time: 5 minutes
Servings: 2

Ingredients:
- Cucumber: 1, peeled, chopped
- Fresh mint leaves: a handful
- Lemon juice: 1 tbsp
- Water: 1 cup
- Honey: 1 tsp
- Ice cubes

Directions:

Introduction: A light and refreshing beverage, perfect for hot days.
Blend all ingredients until smooth. Serve over ice.

Nutritional Information (per serving):
Calories: 45 kcal, Fat: 0g (0 oz), Carbs: 12g (0.42 oz), Protein: 1g (0.04 oz), Sodium: 20mg, Potassium: 50mg, Phosphorus: 10mg

Presentation: Serve in a tall glass, garnished with a mint sprig.

Variation: Add a splash of tonic water for a fizzy twist.

38. GREEN POWER JUICE

Preparation Time: 5 minutes
Servings: 2

Ingredients:
- Spinach leaves: 1 cup
- Green apple: 1, peeled, chopped
- Cucumber: 1, peeled, chopped
- Lemon juice: 1 tbsp
- Water: 1 cup

Directions:
Introduction: A nutrient-rich juice, packed with vitamins and minerals.
Blend all ingredients until smooth. Strain if desired, then serve.

Nutritional Information (per serving):
Calories: 55 kcal, Fat: 0g (0 oz), Carbs: 13g (0.46 oz), Protein: 2g (0.07 oz), Sodium: 30mg, Potassium: 120mg, Phosphorus: 40mg

Presentation: Serve in a glass with a cucumber slice.

Variation: Add a handful of kale for additional nutrients.

39. MELON MINT COOLER

Preparation Time: 5 minutes
Servings: 2

Ingredients:
- Watermelon chunks: 1 cup
- Fresh mint leaves: a handful
- Lemon juice: 1 tbsp
- Water: 1/2 cup
- Ice cubes

Directions:
Introduction: A light and refreshing cooler with a hint of mint.
Blend all ingredients until smooth. Serve over ice.

Nutritional Information (per serving):
Calories: 60 kcal, Fat: 0g (0 oz), Carbs: 15g (0.53 oz), Protein: 1g (0.04 oz), Sodium: 25mg, Potassium: 80mg, Phosphorus: 20mg

Presentation: Serve in a glass with a mint leaf garnish.

Variation: Mix in some honeydew melon for extra sweetness.

40. ORANGE SUNRISE SMOOTHIE

Preparation Time: 5 minutes
Servings: 2

Ingredients:
- Orange juice: 1 cup
- Banana: 1 peeled
- Greek yogurt: 1 cup
- Honey: 1 tbsp

- Ice cubes

Directions:

Introduction: A bright and tangy smoothie, ideal for a morning boost.

Blend all ingredients until smooth. Serve chilled.

Nutritional Information (per serving):

Calories: 180 kcal, Fat: 4g (0.14 oz), Carbs: 35g (1.23 oz), Protein: 7g (0.25 oz), Sodium: 50mg, Potassium: 200mg, Phosphorus: 80mg

Presentation: Serve in a glass with an orange wedge on the rim.

Variation: Use a frozen banana for a thicker consistency.

41. PAPAYA-COCONUT SMOOTHIE

Preparation Time: 5 minutes
Servings: 2

Ingredients:

- Papaya: 1 cup, peeled, chopped
- Coconut milk: 1 cup
- Greek yogurt: 1 cup
- Honey: 1 tbsp
- Ice cubes

Directions:

Introduction: A tropical smoothie with a creamy texture.

Blend all ingredients until smooth. Serve chilled.

Nutritional Information (per serving):

Calories: 170 kcal, Fat: 6g (0.21 oz), Carbs: 25g (0.88 oz), Protein: 6g (0.21 oz), Sodium: 40mg, Potassium: 180mg, Phosphorus: 80mg

Presentation: Serve in a tall glass with a coconut flake garnish.

Variation: Add a tablespoon of chia seeds for extra fiber.

42. PEACH-GINGER SMOOTHIE

Preparation Time: 5 minutes
Servings: 2

Ingredients:

- Peaches: 1 cup, peeled, sliced
- Greek yogurt: 1 cup
- Ginger: 1 tsp grated
- Almond milk: 1/2 cup
- Honey: 1 tsp
- Ice cubes

Directions:

Introduction: A delicious blend of sweet and spicy flavors.

Blend all ingredients until smooth. Serve chilled.

Nutritional Information (per serving):

Calories: 170 kcal, Fat: 4g (0.14 oz), Carbs: 28g (0.99 oz), Protein: 8g (0.28 oz), Sodium: 40mg, Potassium: 180mg, Phosphorus: 80mg

Presentation: Serve in a clear glass with a peach slice on the rim.

Variation: Add a touch of nutmeg for extra warmth.

43. PINEAPPLE-SPINACH SMOOTHIE

Preparation Time: 5 minutes
Servings: 2

Ingredients:
- Pineapple chunks: 1 cup
- Spinach leaves: 1 cup
- Greek yogurt: 1 cup
- Almond milk: 1/2 cup
- Honey: 1 tsp
- Ice cubes

Directions:

Introduction: A refreshing smoothie combining tropical flavors with nutritious greens.
Blend all ingredients until smooth. Serve immediately.

Nutritional Information (per serving):
Calories: 150 kcal, Fat: 3g (0.11 oz), Carbs: 25g (0.88 oz), Protein: 7g (0.25 oz), Sodium: 40mg, Potassium: 160mg, Phosphorus: 70mg

Presentation: Serve in a tall glass with a pineapple chunk on the rim.

Variation: Add a tablespoon of chia seeds for extra fiber.

44. STRAWBERRY-BANANA SHAKE

Preparation Time: 5 minutes
Servings: 2

Ingredients:
- Strawberries: 1 cup
- Banana: 1 peeled
- Almond milk: 1 cup
- Honey: 1 tbsp
- Ice cubes

Directions:

Introduction: A creamy and delicious shake, rich in vitamins.
Blend all ingredients until smooth. Serve immediately.

Nutritional Information (per serving):
Calories: 180 kcal, Fat: 3g (0.11 oz), Carbs: 35g (1.23 oz), Protein: 6g (0.21 oz), Sodium: 40mg, Potassium: 160mg, Phosphorus: 70mg

Presentation: Serve in a glass with a strawberry slice on the rim.

Variation: Add a tablespoon of cocoa powder for a chocolate twist.

45. TROPICAL DELIGHT SMOOTHIE

Preparation Time: 5 minutes
Servings: 2

Ingredients:
- Pineapple chunks: 1 cup
- Coconut milk: 1 cup
- Banana: 1 peeled
- Honey: 1 tsp
- Ice cubes

Directions:

Introduction: A tropical blend of sweet and creamy flavors.
Blend all ingredients until smooth. Serve immediately.

Nutritional Information (per serving):
Calories: 170 kcal, Fat: 6g (0.21 oz), Carbs: 25g (0.88 oz), Protein: 4g (0.14 oz), Sodium: 45mg, Potassium: 160mg, Phosphorus: 70mg

Presentation: Serve in a tall glass with a pineapple chunk on the rim.

Variation: Add a teaspoon of chia seeds for extra fiber.

46. KIWI-SPINACH SMOOTHIE

Preparation Time: 5 minutes
Servings: 2

Ingredients:
- Kiwi: 2, peeled, chopped
- Spinach leaves: 1 cup
- Greek yogurt: 1 cup
- Honey: 1 tbsp
- Ice cubes

Directions:
Introduction: A refreshing blend rich in vitamins and minerals.
Blend all ingredients until smooth. Serve chilled.

Nutritional Information (per serving):
Calories: 140 kcal, Fat: 2g (0.07 oz), Carbs: 27g (0.95 oz), Protein: 8g (0.28 oz), Sodium: 40mg, Potassium: 180mg, Phosphorus: 70mg

Presentation: Serve in a tall glass with a kiwi slice on the rim.

Variation: Add a teaspoon of chia seeds for extra fiber.

47. WATERMELON-MINT SMOOTHIE

Preparation Time: 5 minutes
Servings: 2

Ingredients:
- Watermelon chunks: 1 cup
- Fresh mint leaves: a handful
- Greek yogurt: 1 cup
- Honey: 1 tbsp
- Ice cubes

Directions:
Introduction: A light and refreshing smoothie with a hint of mint.
Blend all ingredients until smooth. Serve chilled.

Nutritional Information (per serving):
Calories: 130 kcal, Fat: 3g (0.11 oz), Carbs: 25g (0.88 oz), Protein: 6g (0.21 oz), Sodium: 35mg, Potassium: 120mg, Phosphorus: 60mg

Presentation: Serve in a clear glass with a mint sprig garnish.

Variation: Add a slice of lime for extra tanginess.

APPLE AND OAT SMOOTHIES

48. CLASSIC APPLE AND OAT SMOOTHIE

Preparation Time: 5 minutes
Servings: 2

Ingredients:
- Apples: 2, cored and sliced
- Rolled oats: 1/4 cup
- Greek yogurt: 1/2 cup
- Honey: 1 tbsp
- Cinnamon: 1/2 tsp
- Water or ice: as needed

Directions:

Blend all ingredients until smooth. Add water or ice to achieve desired consistency.

Nutritional Information (per serving):
Calories: 180 kcal, Protein: 6g (0.21 oz), Carbs: 34g (1.20 oz), Fat: 2g (0.07 oz), Sodium: 30mg, Potassium: 200mg, Phosphorus: 100mg

Storage: Refrigerate any leftovers in a sealed container for up to 24 hours. Shake well before drinking as separation may occur.

49. APPLE, BEET, AND OAT SMOOTHIE

Preparation Time: 5 minutes
Servings: 2

Ingredients:
- Apples: 2, cored and sliced
- Cooked beets: 1/2 cup, peeled and chopped
- Rolled oats: 1/4 cup
- Greek yogurt: 1/2 cup
- Water or ice: as needed

Directions:
Blend all ingredients until smooth. The beets add earthiness and vibrant color.

Nutritional Information (per serving):
Calories: 190 kcal, Protein: 7g (0.25 oz), Carbs: 36g (1.27 oz), Fat: 2g (0.07 oz), Sodium: 40mg, Potassium: 300mg, Phosphorus: 110mg

Storage: This smoothie can be kept in a tightly sealed jar in the refrigerator for up to 24 hours. The beets may settle, so stir well before re-serving.

50. APPLE, CARROT, AND GINGER OAT SMOOTHIE

Preparation Time: 5 minutes
Servings: 2

Ingredients:
- Apples: 2, cored and sliced
- Carrots: 2, peeled and chopped
- Fresh ginger: 1 tsp, grated
- Rolled oats: 1/4 cup
- Greek yogurt: 1/2 cup
- Water or ice: as needed

Directions:
Blend all ingredients until smooth. Ginger adds a spicy kick and digestive benefits.

Nutritional Information (per serving):
Calories: 160 kcal, Protein: 6g (0.21 oz), Carbs: 30g (1.06 oz), Fat: 2g (0.07 oz), Sodium: 35mg, Potassium: 250mg, Phosphorus: 100mg

Storage: Store in the fridge in an airtight container for up to one day. The flavors will intensify, especially the ginger, so it may taste stronger the next day.

51. APPLE, PEAR, AND OAT SMOOTHIE

Preparation Time: 5 minutes
Servings: 2

Ingredients:
- Apples: 1, cored and sliced
- Pears: 1, cored and sliced
- Rolled oats: 1/4 cup
- Greek yogurt: 1/2 cup
- Honey: 1 tsp

- Water or ice: as needed

Directions:
Blend all ingredients until smooth. The pear adds sweetness and a smooth texture.

Nutritional Information (per serving):
Calories: 170 kcal, Protein: 6g (0.21 oz), Carbs: 36g (1.27 oz), Fat: 2g (0.07 oz), Sodium: 25mg, Potassium: 210mg, Phosphorus: 95mg

Storage: Keep leftovers refrigerated in a closed container; consume within 24 hours for best taste and nutrient retention.

52. SPICED APPLE AND OAT SMOOTHIE

Preparation Time: 5 minutes
Servings: 2

Ingredients:
- Apples: 2, cored and sliced
- Rolled oats: 1/4 cup
- Greek yogurt: 1/2 cup
- Maple syrup: 1 tbsp
- Mixed spice (cinnamon, nutmeg, cloves): 1/2 tsp
- Water or ice: as needed

Directions:
Blend all ingredients until smooth. The spices evoke a traditional British pudding flavor.

Nutritional Information (per serving):
Calories: 185 kcal, Protein: 6g (0.21 oz), Carbs: 38g (1.34 oz), Fat: 2g (0.07 oz), Sodium: 30mg, Potassium: 205mg, Phosphorus: 105mg

Storage: Can be refrigerated overnight in a sealed container. Due to the spices, the flavor may enhance over time. Stir well before consuming.

53. APPLE, MINT, AND CUCUMBER OAT SMOOTHIE

Preparation Time: 5 minutes
Servings: 2

Ingredients:
- Apples: 2, cored and sliced
- Cucumber: 1/2, sliced
- Fresh mint leaves: a handful
- Rolled oats: 1/4 cup
- Greek yogurt: 1/2 cup
- Water or ice: as needed

Directions:
Blend all ingredients until smooth. The cucumber and mint offer a refreshing twist.

Nutritional Information (per serving):
Calories: 160 kcal, Protein: 6g (0.21 oz), Carbs: 32g (1.13 oz), Fat: 2g (0.07 oz), Sodium: 25mg, Potassium: 220mg, Phosphorus: 90mg

Storage: Best if consumed immediately, but can be stored in the refrigerator for up to 12 hours. The cucumber might release more water, so stir well before drinking.

54. SCOTTISH APPLE AND BARLEY OAT SMOOTHIE

Preparation Time: 10 minutes
Servings: 2

Ingredients:
- Apples: 2, cored and sliced
- Cooked barley: 1/4 cup
- Rolled oats: 1/4 cup
- Greek yogurt: 1/2 cup
- Honey: 1 tbsp
- Water or ice: as needed

Directions:
Blend all ingredients until smooth. Barley is a staple in Scottish cuisine and adds a unique texture.

Nutritional Information (per serving):
Calories: 190 kcal, Protein: 7g (0.25 oz), Carbs: 40g (1.41 oz), Fat: 2g (0.07 oz), Sodium: 30mg, Potassium: 210mg, Phosphorus: 110mg

Storage: This smoothie should be consumed fresh but can be stored in the fridge for up to 24 hours. The barley may absorb more liquid, so you might need to add a little water or apple juice when you re-serve it.

Chapter 2. Main Courses Recipes

MEAT DISHES

55. BEEF AND VEGETABLE STEW

Preparation Time: 10 minutes
Cooking Time: 1 hour
Servings: 4

Ingredients:
- Beef stew meat: 500g (1.1 lb)
- Carrots: 2, chopped
- Celery: 2 stalks, chopped
- Onion: 1, chopped
- Low-sodium beef broth: 4 cups
- Olive oil: 1 tbsp
- Black pepper: 1/2 tsp

Directions:
Introduction: A hearty stew with a balanced mix of protein and vegetables.
Cooking: Heat oil in a pot, add beef and brown. Add vegetables and broth, simmer for an hour until meat is tender.

Nutritional Information (per serving):
Calories: 250 kcal, Fat: 10g (0.35 oz), Carbs: 10g (0.35 oz), Protein: 30g (1.06 oz), Sodium: 120mg, Potassium: 350mg, Phosphorus: 200mg

Storage: Can be refrigerated for up to 3 days.
Presentation: Serve in bowls, garnished with parsley.
Variation: Substitute turkey for beef for a lighter option.

56. CHICKEN AND LEEK PIE

Preparation Time: 20 minutes
Cooking Time: 40 minutes
Servings: 4

Ingredients:
- Chicken breast: 500g (1.1 lb), cubed
- Leeks: 2, sliced
- Olive oil: 1 tbsp
- Low-sodium chicken broth: 1 cup
- Cornstarch: 2 tbsp
- Water: 1/4 cup
- Wholemeal pie crust: 1

Directions:
Introduction: A creamy, classic dish with a UK twist.
Cooking: Heat oil, add chicken and leeks, sauté until golden. Mix cornstarch with water, stir into broth, add to chicken. Cook until thickened. Place in pie crust, bake until golden brown.

Nutritional Information (per serving):
Calories: 300 kcal, Fat: 12g (0.42 oz), Carbs: 25g (0.88 oz), Protein: 20g (0.71 oz), Sodium: 150mg, Potassium: 200mg, Phosphorus: 150mg

Storage: Best eaten fresh.
Presentation: Serve on plates with a side of steamed vegetables.
Variation: Use puff pastry for a flakier crust.

57. CORNED BEEF HASH

Preparation Time: 10 minutes
Cooking Time: 20 minutes
Servings: 4

Ingredients:
- Corned beef: 400g (0.88 lb), cubed
- Potatoes: 2, peeled, cubed
- Onion: 1, chopped
- Olive oil: 2 tbsp
- Black pepper: 1/2 tsp

Directions:
Introduction: A savory and filling dish, ideal for a hearty meal.
Cooking: Heat oil, add potatoes, cook until golden. Add onion and beef, cook until meat is browned.

Nutritional Information (per serving):
Calories: 280 kcal, Fat: 15g (0.53 oz), Carbs: 20g (0.71 oz), Protein: 20g (0.71 oz), Sodium: 200mg, Potassium: 250mg, Phosphorus: 150mg

Storage: Best eaten fresh.

Presentation: Serve on a plate, garnished with parsley.

Variation: Add bell peppers for extra color and flavor.

58. CUMBERLAND SAUSAGE

Preparation Time: 10 minutes
Cooking Time: 20 minutes
Servings: 4

Ingredients:
- Cumberland sausage: 4 links
- Olive oil: 1 tbsp

Directions:
Introduction: A traditional British sausage with a unique flavor.
Cooking: Heat oil in a pan, add sausages, cook until browned and cooked through.

Nutritional Information (per serving):
Calories: 250 kcal, Fat: 20g (0.71 oz), Carbs: 5g (0.18 oz), Protein: 15g (0.53 oz), Sodium: 150mg, Potassium: 100mg, Phosphorus: 80mg

Storage: Best eaten fresh.

Presentation: Serve on a plate with a side of mashed potatoes.

Variation: Serve with sautéed onions for extra flavor.

59. HAGGIS

Preparation Time: 15 minutes
Cooking Time: 1 hour
Servings: 4

Ingredients:
- Minced lamb: 500g (1.1 lb)
- Onion: 1, chopped
- Oats: 1 cup
- Black pepper: 1 tsp
- Olive oil: 2 tbsp

Directions:
Introduction: A traditional Scottish dish, adapted for renal patients.
Cooking: Heat oil, add lamb and onion, cook until browned. Mix in oats and pepper, shape into a loaf, and bake until fully cooked.

Nutritional Information (per serving):
Calories: 300 kcal, Fat: 15g (0.53 oz), Carbs: 15g (0.53 oz), Protein: 25g (0.88 oz), Sodium: 100mg, Potassium: 250mg, Phosphorus: 150mg

Storage: Can be refrigerated for up to 3 days.

Presentation: Serve on a plate with a side of mashed turnips.

Variation: Add some herbs for extra flavor.

60. ROAST BEEF

Preparation Time: 15 minutes
Cooking Time: 1 hour
Servings: 4

Ingredients:
- Beef roast: 1 kg (2.2 lb)
- Olive oil: 2 tbsp
- Black pepper: 1 tsp

Directions:
Introduction: A classic British dish for special occasions.
Cooking: Rub roast with oil and pepper, cook in the oven until desired doneness.

Nutritional Information (per serving):
Calories: 350 kcal, Fat: 25g (0.88 oz), Carbs: 0g (0 oz), Protein: 30g (1.06 oz), Sodium: 100mg, Potassium: 300mg, Phosphorus: 200mg

Storage: Can be refrigerated for up to 3 days.

Presentation: Serve on a plate with a side of steamed vegetables.

Variation: Use garlic and rosemary for extra flavor.

61. SHEPHERD'S PIE

Preparation Time: 20 minutes
Cooking Time: 40 minutes
Servings: 4

Ingredients:
- Minced lamb: 500g (1.1 lb)
- Onion: 1, chopped
- Carrots: 2, chopped
- Peas: 1 cup
- Low-sodium chicken broth: 1 cup
- Olive oil: 2 tbsp
- Potatoes: 4, mashed

Directions:
Introduction: A hearty and classic British dish.
Cooking: Heat oil, add lamb and onion, cook until browned. Add vegetables and broth, simmer. Layer in a baking dish, top with mashed potatoes, bake until golden brown.

Nutritional Information (per serving):
Calories: 400 kcal, Fat: 20g (0.71 oz), Carbs: 40g (1.41 oz), Protein: 20g (0.71 oz), Sodium: 150mg, Potassium: 300mg, Phosphorus: 200mg

Storage: Can be refrigerated for up to 2 days.

Presentation: Serve on a plate with a side salad.

Variation: Substitute turkey for lamb for a lighter option.

62. STEAK AND KIDNEY PIE

Preparation Time: 20 minutes
Cooking Time: 1 hour
Servings: 4

Ingredients:
- Beef stew meat: 300g (0.66 lb)
- Lamb kidneys: 200g (0.44 lb), chopped
- Onion: 1, chopped
- Low-sodium beef broth: 1 cup
- Olive oil: 1 tbsp
- Cornstarch: 2 tbsp
- Water: 1/4 cup

- Wholemeal pie crust: 1

Directions:

Introduction: A classic British pie with a rich and hearty filling.

Cooking: Heat oil, add meat and onion, brown. Mix cornstarch with water, add to broth, pour into meat, cook until thickened. Place in pie crust, bake until golden.

Nutritional Information (per serving):
Calories: 350 kcal, Fat: 15g (0.53 oz), Carbs: 30g (1.06 oz), Protein: 25g (0.88 oz), Sodium: 150mg, Potassium: 200mg, Phosphorus: 150mg

Storage: Best eaten fresh.

Presentation: Serve on a plate with a side of steamed peas.

Variation: Use chicken instead of kidneys for a lighter taste.

63. TOAD IN THE HOLE

Preparation Time: 10 minutes
Cooking Time: 30 minutes
Servings: 4

Ingredients:
- Cumberland sausage: 4 links
- Flour: 1 cup
- Milk: 1 cup
- Egg: 1
- Olive oil: 1 tbsp

Directions:

Introduction: A traditional British dish with a savory batter.

Cooking: Brown the sausages in oil. Mix flour, milk, and egg to form a batter. Pour batter into a baking dish, add sausages, and bake until golden brown.

Nutritional Information (per serving):
Calories: 250 kcal, Fat: 12g (0.42 oz), Carbs: 25g (0.88 oz), Protein: 10g (0.35 oz), Sodium: 150mg, Potassio: 200mg, Fosforo: 80mg

Storage: Best eaten fresh.

Presentation: Serve on a plate with a side of steamed vegetables.

Variation: Use chicken sausage for a lighter option.

64. YORKSHIRE PUDDING WITH BEEF

Preparation Time: 10 minutes
Cooking Time: 30 minutes
Servings: 4

Ingredients:
- Beef roast: 400g (0.88 lb), sliced
- Flour: 1 cup
- Milk: 1 cup
- Egg: 1
- Olive oil: 2 tbsp

Directions:

Introduction: A traditional British dish, combining tender beef with savory batter.

Cooking: Mix flour, milk, and egg to form a batter. Pour into a muffin tin, add beef slices, and bake until golden brown.

Nutritional Information (per serving):
Calories: 300 kcal, Fat: 15g (0.53 oz), Carbs: 30g (1.06 oz), Protein: 15g (0.53 oz), Sodium: 120mg, Potassio: 200mg, Fosforo: 100mg

Storage: Best eaten fresh.

Presentation: Serve on a plate, garnished with parsley.

Variation: Use turkey for a lighter option.

FISH DISHES

65. BAKED COD WITH HERB CRUST

Preparation Time: 10 minutes
Cooking Time: 20 minutes
Servings: 4

Ingredients:
- Cod fillets: 4
- Olive oil: 2 tbsp
- Breadcrumbs: 1/2 cup
- Parsley: 2 tbsp, chopped
- Lemon zest: 1 tsp
- Black pepper: 1/2 tsp

Directions:
Introduction: A light, flavorful dish with a fresh herb crust.
Cooking: Mix breadcrumbs, parsley, lemon zest, and pepper. Coat fillets with oil and press breadcrumb mixture on top. Bake until fish flakes easily.

Nutritional Information (per serving):
Calories: 200 kcal, Fat: 8g (0.28 oz), Carbs: 10g (0.35 oz), Protein: 25g (0.88 oz), Sodium: 80mg, Potassio: 250mg, Fosforo: 150mg

Storage: Best eaten fresh.
Presentation: Serve on a plate with a side of steamed vegetables.
Variation: Use panko breadcrumbs for extra crunch.

66. FISH AND CHIPS

Preparation Time: 15 minutes
Cooking Time: 20 minutes
Servings: 4

Ingredients:
- White fish fillets: 4
- Flour: 1 cup
- Sparkling water: 1 cup
- Potatoes: 4, peeled, sliced
- Olive oil: 2 tbsp

Directions:
Introduction: A classic British dish, made lighter for renal patients.
Cooking: Coat fillets in flour, dip in sparkling water, fry until golden brown. Bake sliced potatoes until crisp.

Nutritional Information (per serving):
Calories: 300 kcal, Fat: 12g (0.42 oz), Carbs: 40g (1.41 oz), Protein: 20g (0.71 oz), Sodium: 120mg, Potassio: 300mg, Fosforo: 150mg

Storage: Best eaten fresh.
Presentation: Serve on a plate with a side of mushy peas.
Variation: Bake the fish instead of frying for a lighter option.

67. GRILLED MACKEREL

Preparation Time: 10 minutes
Cooking Time: 15 minutes
Servings: 4

Ingredients:

- Mackerel fillets: 4
- Olive oil: 2 tbsp
- Black pepper: 1 tsp
- Lemon juice: 1 tbsp

Directions:

Introduction: A nutritious and simple dish, rich in omega-3s.

Cooking: Brush fillets with oil, season with pepper, and grill until cooked through. Drizzle with lemon juice.

Nutritional Information (per serving):
Calories: 250 kcal, Fat: 15g (0.53 oz), Carbs: 0g (0 oz), Protein: 25g (0.88 oz), Sodium: 80mg, Potassio: 200mg, Fosforo: 100mg

Storage: Best eaten fresh.

Presentation: Serve on a plate with a side of steamed greens.

Variation: Marinate in herbs for extra flavor.

68. HADDOCK CHOWDER

Preparation Time: 10 minutes
Cooking Time: 30 minutes
Servings: 4

Ingredients:
- Haddock fillets: 500g (1.1 lb), chopped
- Onion: 1, chopped
- Celery: 2 stalks, chopped
- Low-sodium fish broth: 4 cups
- Olive oil: 1 tbsp
- Black pepper: 1/2 tsp

Directions:

Introduction: A hearty and warming chowder, adapted for renal patients.

Cooking: Heat oil, add onion and celery, sauté. Add fish and broth, simmer until fish flakes easily.

Nutritional Information (per serving):
Calories: 180 kcal, Fat: 5g (0.18 oz), Carbs: 10g (0.35 oz), Protein: 25g (0.88 oz), Sodium: 120mg, Potassio: 200mg, Fosforo: 100mg

Storage: Can be refrigerated for up to 2 days.

Presentation: Serve in bowls, garnished with parsley.

Variation: Add corn for extra texture.

69. KEDGEREE

Preparation Time: 10 minutes
Cooking Time: 20 minutes
Servings: 4

Ingredients:
- Smoked haddock: 500g (1.1 lb)
- Rice: 1 cup, cooked
- Eggs: 2, hard-boiled, chopped
- Olive oil: 2 tbsp
- Curry powder: 1 tsp

Directions:

Introduction: A traditional British dish with Indian influence, made renal-friendly.

Cooking: Heat oil, add haddock, cook until flaked. Mix with rice, eggs, and curry powder.

Nutritional Information (per serving):
Calories: 250 kcal, Fat: 10g (0.35 oz), Carbs: 30g (1.06 oz), Protein: 20g (0.71 oz), Sodium: 150mg, Potassio: 200mg, Fosforo: 100mg

Storage: Can be refrigerated for up to 2 days.

Presentation: Serve on a plate, garnished with lemon wedges.

Variation: Substitute chicken for haddock for a different twist.

70. LEMON BAKED SALMON

Preparation Time: 10 minutes
Cooking Time: 20 minutes
Servings: 4

Ingredients:
- Salmon fillets: 4
- Olive oil: 2 tbsp
- Lemon juice: 2 tbsp
- Black pepper: 1/2 tsp

Directions:
Introduction: A light and flavorful dish, packed with omega-3s.
Cooking: Coat salmon in oil, drizzle with lemon juice, and sprinkle with pepper. Bake until cooked through.

Nutritional Information (per serving):
Calories: 280 kcal, Fat: 15g (0.53 oz), Carbs: 0g (0 oz), Protein: 30g (1.06 oz), Sodium: 80mg, Potassio: 200mg, Fosforo: 100mg

Storage: Best eaten fresh.
Presentation: Serve on a plate with a side of steamed vegetables.
Variation: Add dill for extra flavor.

71. POACHED HADDOCK WITH DILL SAUCE

Preparation Time: 10 minutes
Cooking Time: 15 minutes
Servings: 4

Ingredients:
- Haddock fillets: 4
- Low-sodium fish broth: 2 cups
- Dill: 2 tbsp, chopped
- Greek yogurt: 1/2 cup
- Lemon juice: 1 tbsp

Directions:
Introduction: A delicate dish with a creamy dill sauce.
Cooking: Poach haddock in broth until cooked through. Mix dill, yogurt, and lemon juice, pour over fish.

Nutritional Information (per serving):
Calories: 220 kcal, Fat: 6g (0.21 oz), Carbs: 5g (0.18 oz), Protein: 30g (1.06 oz), Sodium: 100mg, Potassio: 200mg, Fosforo: 150mg

Storage: Best eaten fresh.
Presentation: Serve on a plate with a side of boiled potatoes.
Variation: Use parsley instead of dill for a different flavor.

72. SCOTTISH FISH PIE

Preparation Time: 15 minutes
Cooking Time: 40 minutes
Servings: 4

Ingredients:
- White fish fillets: 500g (1.1 lb), chopped
- Low-sodium fish broth: 1 cup
- Cornstarch: 2 tbsp
- Water: 1/4 cup
- Potatoes: 4, mashed
- Olive oil: 2 tbsp

Directions:

Introduction: A traditional Scottish dish, adapted for renal patients.
Cooking: Mix cornstarch with water, stir into broth, add fish, simmer until thickened. Layer in a baking dish, top with mashed potatoes, bake until golden brown.

Nutritional Information (per serving):
Calories: 300 kcal, Fat: 10g (0.35 oz), Carbs: 40g (1.41 oz), Protein: 20g (0.71 oz), Sodium: 100mg, Potassio: 200mg, Fosforo: 150mg

Storage: Can be refrigerated for up to 2 days.

Presentation: Serve on a plate with a side of steamed carrots.

Variation: Use sweet potatoes for a different twist.

73. SMOKED SALMON SALAD

Preparation Time: 10 minutes
Servings: 4

Ingredients:
- Smoked salmon: 200g (0.44 lb), sliced
- Mixed greens: 4 cups
- Olive oil: 2 tbsp
- Lemon juice: 2 tbsp
- Black pepper: 1/2 tsp

Directions:
Introduction: A light and refreshing dish, rich in omega-3s.
Assemblage: Toss greens with oil, lemon juice, and pepper. Top with salmon slices.

Nutritional Information (per serving):
Calories: 180 kcal, Fat: 10g (0.35 oz), Carbs: 5g (0.18 oz), Protein: 15g (0.53 oz), Sodium: 70mg, Potassio: 120mg, Fosforo: 80mg

Storage: Best eaten fresh.

Presentation: Serve on a plate, garnished with a lemon wedge.

Variation: Add avocado slices for extra creaminess.

74. SOLE MEUNIÈRE

Preparation Time: 10 minutes
Cooking Time: 15 minutes
Servings: 4

Ingredients:
- Sole fillets: 4
- Flour: 1/2 cup
- Olive oil: 2 tbsp
- Lemon juice: 1 tbsp
- Black pepper: 1/4 tsp

Directions:
Introduction: A classic British dish, light and flavorful.
Cooking: Coat fillets in flour, cook in oil until golden brown. Drizzle with lemon juice and sprinkle with pepper.

Nutritional Information (per serving):
Calories: 200 kcal, Fat: 10g (0.35 oz), Carbs: 10g (0.35 oz), Protein: 20g (0.71 oz), Sodium: 90mg, Potassio: 150mg, Fosforo: 100mg

Storage: Best eaten fresh.

Presentation: Serve on a plate with a side of steamed greens.

Variation: Use lime juice instead of lemon for a different twist.

VEGETARIAN DISHES

75. BAKED STUFFED PEPPERS

Preparation Time: 15 minutes
Cooking Time: 30 minutes
Servings: 4

Ingredients:
- Bell peppers: 4, halved and seeded
- Brown rice: 1 cup, cooked
- Black beans: 1 cup, rinsed and drained
- Corn: 1/2 cup
- Onions: 1/2 cup, diced
- Low-sodium cheese: 1/2 cup, grated
- Olive oil: 1 tbsp

Directions:
Introduction: Colorful peppers stuffed with a hearty mix of rice and vegetables.
Cooking: Combine rice, beans, corn, and onions. Stuff into pepper halves, top with cheese, drizzle with oil, and bake until peppers are tender.

Nutritional Information (per serving):
Calories: 250 kcal, Fat: 8g (0.28 oz), Carbs: 38g (1.34 oz), Protein: 10g (0.35 oz), Sodium: 120mg, Potassium: 300mg, Phosphorus: 100mg

Presentation: Serve hot, garnished with fresh cilantro.
Variation: Add chopped tomatoes for extra juiciness.

76. CAULIFLOWER STEAK

Preparation Time: 10 minutes
Cooking Time: 20 minutes
Servings: 4

Ingredients:
- Cauliflower: 1 large, sliced into 4 steaks
- Olive oil: 2 tbsp
- Paprika: 1 tsp
- Black pepper: 1/2 tsp

Directions:
Introduction: Thick slices of cauliflower grilled to perfection.
Cooking: Brush each cauliflower steak with oil, season with paprika and pepper, and grill until tender.

Nutritional Information (per serving):
Calories: 120 kcal, Fat: 7g (0.25 oz), Carbs: 12g (0.42 oz), Protein: 4g (0.14 oz), Sodium: 30mg, Potassium: 300mg, Phosphorus: 100mg

Presentation: Serve with a drizzle of tahini sauce.
Variation: Add turmeric for a golden color and health boost.

77. CHEESY VEGETABLE CASSEROLE

Preparation Time: 15 minutes
Cooking Time: 35 minutes
Servings: 4

Ingredients:
- Mixed vegetables: 4 cups (carrots, broccoli, zucchini)
- Low-sodium cheese: 1 cup, grated
- Olive oil: 1 tbsp
- Garlic powder: 1 tsp

Directions:
Introduction: A creamy, cheesy delight with a medley of vegetables.
Cooking: Mix vegetables with cheese and garlic powder, drizzle with oil, and bake until golden and bubbly.

Nutritional Information (per serving):
Calories: 200 kcal, Fat: 12g (0.42 oz), Carbs: 15g (0.53 oz), Protein: 8g (0.28 oz), Sodium: 100mg, Potassium: 250mg, Phosphorus: 150mg

Presentation: Serve hot, topped with more melted cheese if desired.

Variation: Sprinkle with breadcrumbs for a crunchy topping.

78. CHICKPEA CURRY

Preparation Time: 10 minutes
Cooking Time: 25 minutes
Servings: 4

Ingredients:
- Chickpeas: 2 cups, cooked
- Coconut milk: 1 cup
- Onion: 1, diced
- Tomato: 1, diced
- Curry powder: 1 tbsp
- Olive oil: 1 tbsp

Directions:
Introduction: A rich and flavorful curry with a creamy texture.
Cooking: Sauté onions in oil, add tomatoes and curry powder, stir in chickpeas and coconut milk, simmer until thickened.

Nutritional Information (per serving):
Calories: 300 kcal, Fat: 15g (0.53 oz), Carbs: 35g (1.23 oz), Protein: 8g (0.28 oz), Sodium: 80mg, Potassium: 350mg, Phosphorus: 120mg

Presentation: Serve with steamed rice or flatbread.

Variation: Add spinach for an extra dose of greens.

79. EGGPLANT PARMESAN

Preparation Time: 15 minutes
Cooking Time: 30 minutes
Servings: 4

Ingredients:
- Eggplant: 2, sliced
- Low-sodium tomato sauce: 2 cups
- Low-sodium mozzarella: 1 cup, sliced
- Olive oil: 1 tbsp
- Basil: 1 tbsp, chopped

Directions:
Introduction: A classic Italian dish made kidney-friendly.
Cooking: Layer eggplant slices with tomato sauce and mozzarella, drizzle with oil, bake until cheese is bubbly and eggplant is tender.

Nutritional Information (per serving):
Calories: 200 kcal, Fat: 10g (0.35 oz), Carbs: 20g (0.71 oz), Protein: 10g (0.35 oz), Sodium: 100mg, Potassium: 300mg, Phosphorus: 150mg

Presentation: Serve hot, garnished with fresh basil.

Variation: Add a layer of cooked spinach between the eggplant slices.

80. LENTIL STEW

Preparation Time: 10 minutes
Cooking Time: 40 minutes
Servings: 4

Ingredients:
- Lentils: 2 cups, rinsed
- Carrots: 2, diced
- Celery: 2 stalks, diced
- Onion: 1, diced

- Low-sodium vegetable broth: 4 cups
- Olive oil: 1 tbsp
- Thyme: 1 tsp

Directions:
Introduction: A hearty stew packed with nutrients and flavors.
Cooking: Sauté onions, carrots, and celery in oil, add lentils and broth, simmer until lentils are tender.

Nutritional Information (per serving):
Calories: 250 kcal, Fat: 5g (0.18 oz), Carbs: 40g (1.41 oz), Protein: 15g (0.53 oz), Sodium: 80mg, Potassium: 400mg, Phosphorus: 150mg

Presentation: Serve in bowls, garnished with a sprig of thyme.
Variation: Add diced tomatoes for extra zest.

81. MUSHROOM RISOTTO

Preparation Time: 10 minutes
Cooking Time: 25 minutes
Servings: 4

Ingredients:
- Arborio rice: 1 cup
- Mushrooms: 2 cups, sliced
- Onion: 1, chopped
- Low-sodium vegetable broth: 4 cups
- Olive oil: 2 tbsp
- Black pepper: 1/2 tsp

Directions:
Introduction: A creamy and luxurious risotto, perfect for a cozy dinner.
Cooking: Sauté onions and mushrooms in oil, add rice, gradually stir in broth until absorbed and rice is creamy.

Nutritional Information (per serving):
Calories: 280 kcal, Fat: 8g (0.28 oz), Carbs: 45g (1.59 oz), Protein: 8g (0.28 oz), Sodium: 70mg, Potassium: 200mg, Phosphorus: 100mg

Presentation: Serve in shallow bowls, garnished with parsley.
Variation: Add a splash of white wine to the rice before adding broth for added flavor.

82. QUINOA AND VEGETABLE STIR-FRY

Preparation Time: 10 minutes
Cooking Time: 20 minutes
Servings: 4

Ingredients:
- Quinoa: 1 cup, cooked
- Mixed vegetables: 3 cups (bell peppers, zucchini, carrots)
- Soy sauce (low-sodium): 2 tbsp
- Olive oil: 1 tbsp
- Garlic: 1 clove, minced

Directions:
Introduction: A quick and colorful stir-fry, rich in protein and fiber.
Cooking: Sauté vegetables and garlic in oil, add cooked quinoa, stir in soy sauce, cook until vegetables are tender.

Nutritional Information (per serving):
Calories: 220 kcal, Fat: 7g (0.25 oz), Carbs: 32g (1.13 oz), Protein: 8g (0.28 oz), Sodium: 50mg, Potassium: 300mg, Phosphorus: 150mg

Presentation: Serve hot, topped with chopped scallions.

Variation: Add tofu for extra protein.

83. RATATOUILLE

Preparation Time: 15 minutes
Cooking Time: 40 minutes
Servings: 4

Ingredients:
- Eggplant: 1, cubed
- Zucchini: 2, cubed
- Bell peppers: 2, cubed
- Tomatoes: 3, diced
- Onion: 1, chopped
- Garlic: 2 cloves, minced
- Olive oil: 2 tbsp
- Thyme: 1 tsp

Directions:
Introduction: A French classic with a medley of summer vegetables.
Cooking: Sauté onions and garlic in oil, add vegetables, cook until tender and flavorful.

Nutritional Information (per serving):
Calories: 150 kcal, Fat: 7g (0.25 oz), Carbs: 20g (0.71 oz), Protein: 4g (0.14 oz), Sodium: 50mg, Potassium: 350mg, Phosphorus: 100mg

Presentation: Serve hot, garnished with fresh thyme.

Variation: Add a splash of balsamic vinegar for extradepth of flavor.

84. VEGETABLE PAELLA

Preparation Time: 15 minutes
Cooking Time: 30 minutes
Servings: 4

Ingredients:
- Arborio rice: 1 cup
- Mixed vegetables: 4 cups (peas, bell peppers, artichokes)
- Saffron: 1 tsp
- Low-sodium vegetable broth: 4 cups
- Olive oil: 2 tbsp
- Garlic: 2 cloves, minced

Directions:
Introduction: A vibrant Spanish dish, bursting with flavors and colors.
Cooking: Sauté garlic in oil, add rice, vegetables, saffron, and broth, simmer until rice is tender.

Nutritional Information (per serving):
Calories: 270 kcal, Fat: 7g (0.25 oz), Carbs: 45g (1.59 oz), Protein: 8g (0.28 oz), Sodium: 80mg, Potassium: 250mg, Phosphorus: 100mg

Presentation: Serve in a large dish, garnished with lemon wedges.

Variation: Add chickpeas for added protein and texture.

Chapter 3. BONUS. Air Fryer Main Courses

MEAT DISHES

85. AIR FRYER ROAST CHICKEN

Preparation Time: 10 minutes
Cooking Time: 45 minutes
Servings: 4

Ingredients:
- Whole chicken: 1 (about 3 lbs)
- Olive oil: 2 tbsp
- Thyme: 1 tsp
- Rosemary: 1 tsp
- Black pepper: 1/2 tsp

Directions:
Introduction: A classic roast chicken with a crispy skin and juicy interior, cooked in an Air Fryer.
Cooking: Rub the chicken with olive oil, thyme, rosemary, and pepper. Cook in the Air Fryer at 360°F until the skin is golden and the meat reaches an internal temperature of 165°F.

Nutritional Information (per serving):
Calories: 240 kcal, Fat: 14g (0.49 oz), Carbs: 0g, Protein: 28g (0.99 oz), Sodium: 120mg, Potassium: 250mg, Phosphorus: 220mg

Presentation: Serve on a platter, garnished with fresh herbs.
Variation: Add garlic powder for an extra flavor boost.

86. AIR FRYER BEEF STEAK

Preparation Time: 5 minutes
Cooking Time: 15 minutes
Servings: 2

Ingredients:
- Beef steak: 2 (6 oz each)
- Olive oil: 1 tbsp
- Black pepper: 1/2 tsp

Directions:
Introduction: Perfectly cooked steak with a crispy exterior and tender interior.
Cooking: Brush the steak with olive oil and season with pepper. Cook in the Air Fryer at 400°F for about 7-8 minutes per side for medium-rare.

Nutritional Information (per serving):
Calories: 300 kcal, Fat: 20g, Carbs: 0g, Protein: 28g, Sodium: 60mg, Potassium: 300mg, Phosphorus: 250mg

Presentation: Serve with a side of air-fried asparagus.
Variation: Add a sprinkle of dried rosemary for an aromatic touch.

87. AIR FRYER PORK CHOPS

Preparation Time: 5 minutes
Cooking Time: 20 minutes
Servings: 4

Ingredients:
- Pork chops: 4 (1 inch thick)

- Olive oil: 2 tbsp
- Garlic powder: 1 tsp
- Black pepper: 1/2 tsp

Directions:

Introduction: Juicy pork chops with a golden crust, made healthier in an Air Fryer.

Cooking: Season pork chops with garlic powder and pepper, brush with olive oil. Cook in the Air Fryer at 380°F until the chops are cooked through.

Nutritional Information (per serving):

Calories: 220 kcal, Fat: 12g (0.42 oz), Carbs: 0g, Protein: 26g (0.92 oz), Sodium: 70mg, Potassium: 350mg, Phosphorus: 200mg

Presentation: Serve on a plate, accompanied by a light salad.

Variation: Add a pinch of smoked paprika for a smoky flavor.

88. AIR FRYER LAMB KEBABS

Preparation Time: 15 minutes (plus marinating time)
Cooking Time: 10 minutes
Servings: 4

Ingredients:

- Lamb: 1 lb, cubed
- Yogurt: 1/2 cup
- Mint: 2 tbsp, chopped
- Cumin: 1 tsp
- Olive oil: 1 tbsp
- Lemon juice: 1 tbsp

Directions:

Introduction: Flavorful lamb kebabs marinated in a mint-yogurt sauce and cooked to perfection.

Cooking: Marinate lamb cubes in yogurt, mint, cumin, and lemon juice for at least 2 hours. Thread onto skewers, brush with oil, and cook in the Air Fryer at 400°F until browned.

Nutritional Information (per serving):

Calories: 280 kcal, Fat: 18g (0.63 oz), Carbs: 3g (0.11 oz), Protein: 26g (0.92 oz), Sodium: 80mg, Potassium: 300mg, Phosphorus: 250mg

Presentation: Serve skewered with slices of onion and bell pepper.

Variation: Add chili flakes for a spicy kick.

89. AIR FRYER TURKEY MEATBALLS

Preparation Time: 10 minutes
Cooking Time: 15 minutes
Servings: 4

Ingredients:

- Ground turkey: 1 lb
- Onion: 1/4 cup, finely chopped
- Parsley: 2 tbsp, chopped
- Egg: 1, beaten
- Olive oil: 1 tbsp
- Black pepper: 1/2 tsp

Directions:

Introduction: Light and savory turkey meatballs, ideal for a healthy meal.

Cooking: Mix turkey, onion, parsley, egg, and pepper. Form into balls, brush with oil, and cook in the Air Fryer at 360°F until golden.

Nutritional Information (per serving):

Calories: 180 kcal, Fat: 10g (0.35 oz), Carbs: 2g (0.07 oz), Protein: 20g (0.71 oz), Sodium: 80mg, Potassium: 250mg, Phosphorus: 180mg

Presentation: Serve with a dipping sauce or over whole grain pasta.

Variation: Add grated zucchini for added moisture and nutrients.

90. AIR FRYER DUCK BREASTS

Preparation Time: 5 minutes
Cooking Time: 20 minutes
Servings: 2

Ingredients:
- Duck breasts: 2, skin scored
- Olive oil: 1 tbsp
- Black pepper: 1/4 tsp

Directions:
Introduction: Crispy-skinned duck breasts, cooked to juicy perfection in an Air Fryer.
Cooking: Rub duck breasts with olive oil and season with pepper. Place in the Air Fryer skin-side down at 360°F for 10 minutes, then flip and cook for another 10 minutes.

Nutritional Information (per serving):
Calories: 290 kcal, Fat: 22g (0.78 oz), Carbs: 0g, Protein: 22g (0.78 oz), Sodium: 60mg, Potassium: 300mg, Phosphorus: 210mg

Presentation: Serve with a side of steamed green beans.

Variation: Add a balsamic glaze for a touch of sweetness.

91. AIR FRYER CORNISH HEN

Preparation Time: 10 minutes
Cooking Time: 30 minutes
Servings: 2

Ingredients:
- Cornish hens: 2, halved
- Olive oil: 2 tbsp
- Thyme: 1 tsp
- Black pepper: 1/2 tsp

Directions:
Introduction: Perfectly roasted Cornish hens with a herbaceous aroma, ideal for a special dinner.
Cooking: Rub hens with olive oil, thyme, and pepper. Cook in the Air Fryer at 360°F for 30 minutes or until the skin is crispy and the meat is cooked through.

Nutritional Information (per serving):
Calories: 350 kcal, Fat: 25g, Carbs: 0g, Protein: 30g, Sodium: 80mg, Potassium: 320mg, Phosphorus: 230mg

Presentation: Serve on a platter garnished with lemon slices.

Variation: Stuff the hens with a mixture of wild rice and cranberries for added flavor and texture.

92. AIR FRYER VENISON STEAKS

Preparation Time: 5 minutes
Cooking Time: 12 minutes
Servings: 2

Ingredients:
- Venison steaks: 2 (6 oz each)
- Olive oil: 1 tbsp
- Black pepper: 1/2 tsp
- Juniper berries: crushed, 1 tsp

Directions:
Introduction: Tender venison steaks with a distinctive juniper flavor, cooked swiftly in an Air Fryer.
Cooking: Brush steaks with olive oil and season with black pepper and crushed juniper berries. Cook in the Air Fryer at 400°F for 6 minutes per side.

Nutritional Information (per serving):
Calories: 260 kcal, Fat: 8g (0.28 oz), Carbs: 0g, Protein: 40g (1.41 oz), Sodium: 70mg, Potassium: 380mg, Phosphorus: 300mg

Presentation: Serve with a side of roasted root vegetables.

Variation: Marinate the steaks in red wine and garlic prior to cooking for deeper flavor.

93. AIR FRYER RABBIT LEGS

Preparation Time: 10 minutes
Cooking Time: 25 minutes
Servings: 4

Ingredients:
- Rabbit legs: 4
- Olive oil: 2 tbsp
- Rosemary: 1 tbsp, chopped
- Garlic: minced, 1 tbsp
- Black pepper: 1/2 tsp

Directions:
Introduction: Delicately flavored rabbit legs with a hint of rosemary, ideal for a gourmet meal.
Cooking: Marinate rabbit legs in olive oil, rosemary, garlic, and pepper for at least 1 hour. Cook in the Air Fryer at 380°F for 25 minutes.

Nutritional Information (per serving):
Calories: 220 kcal, Fat: 12g (0.42 oz), Carbs: 0g, Protein: 28g (0.99 oz), Sodium: 65mg, Potassium: 350mg, Phosphorus: 250mg

Presentation: Serve on a platter, garnished with additional rosemary sprigs.

Variation: Add a splash of lemon juice to the marinade for a citrusy note.

94. AIR FRYER MEATLOAF

Preparation Time: 10 minutes
Cooking Time: 20 minutes
Servings: 4

Ingredients:
- Ground beef: 1 lb
- Onion: 1/2 cup, finely chopped
- Carrot: 1/4 cup, grated
- Egg: 1
- Worcestershire sauce: 1 tbsp
- Olive oil: 1 tbsp
- Black pepper: 1/2 tsp

Directions:
Introduction: A classic meatloaf with a modern twist, cooked in an Air Fryer for a healthier option.
Cooking: Mix ground beef, onion, carrot, egg, Worcestershire sauce, and pepper. Form into a loaf, brush with olive oil, and cook in the Air Fryer at 360°F for 20 minutes.

Nutritional Information (per serving):
Calories: 280 kcal, Fat: 18g (0.63 oz), Carbs: 5g (0.18 oz), Protein: 26g (0.92 oz), Sodium: 120mg, Potassium: 320mg, Phosphorus: 240mg

Presentation: Slice and serve on a plate with a side of mashed potatoes.

Variation: Add chopped bell peppers for added color and nutrients.

FISH DISHES

95. AIR FRYER TROUT WITH ALMONDS

Preparation Time: 5 minutes
Cooking Time: 10 minutes
Servings: 4

Ingredients:
- Trout fillets: 4 (6 oz each)
- Sliced almonds: 1/4 cup
- Olive oil: 2 tbsp
- Lemon zest: 1 tsp
- Parsley: 2 tbsp, chopped
- Black pepper: 1/4 tsp

Directions:
Introduction: Delicate trout fillets topped with crunchy almonds.
Cooking: Brush trout with olive oil, season with black pepper and lemon zest. Place in the Air Fryer, sprinkle with almonds, and cook at 350°F until the fish is flaky.

Nutritional Information (per serving):
Calories: 280 kcal, Fat: 18g (0.63 oz), Carbs: 2g (0.07 oz), Protein: 26g (0.92 oz), Sodium: 65mg, Potassium: 450mg, Phosphorus: 300mg

Presentation: Serve garnished with fresh parsley and lemon slices.

Variation: Add a drizzle of honey before cooking for a sweet touch.

96. AIR FRYER LEMON SOLE

Preparation Time: 5 minutes
Cooking Time: 12 minutes
Servings: 4

Ingredients:
- Sole fillets: 4 (5 oz each)
- Olive oil: 2 tbsp
- Lemon juice: 2 tbsp
- Dill: 1 tbsp, chopped
- Black pepper: 1/4 tsp

Directions:
Introduction: A simple yet flavorful fish dish with a lemon-dill seasoning.
Cooking: Coat sole in olive oil and lemon juice, season with dill and black pepper. Cook in the Air Fryer at 360°F until tender.

Nutritional Information (per serving):
Calories: 180 kcal, Fat: 10g (0.35 oz), Carbs: 1g (0.04 oz), Protein: 20g (0.71 oz), Sodium: 75mg, Potassium: 350mg, Phosphorus: 250mg

Presentation: Serve with a side of air-fried asparagus.

Variation: Sprinkle with capers before serving for an extra burst of flavor.

97. AIR FRYER HERBED COD

Preparation Time: 10 minutes
Cooking Time: 15 minutes
Servings: 4

Ingredients:
- Cod fillets: 4 (6 oz each)
- Olive oil: 2 tbsp
- Mixed herbs (thyme, rosemary, parsley): 2 tbsp, chopped
- Garlic: 2 cloves, minced
- Black pepper: 1/4 tsp

Directions:

Introduction: Flavor-packed cod fillets with a medley of herbs.

Cooking: Mix olive oil, herbs, garlic, and black pepper. Brush on cod fillets. Cook in the Air Fryer at 370°F for 15 minutes.

Nutritional Information (per serving):
Calories: 200 kcal, Fat: 7g (0.25 oz), Carbs: 0g, Protein: 30g (1.06 oz), Sodium: 70mg, Potassium: 500mg, Phosphorus: 280mg

Presentation: Serve immediately, garnished with additional herbs.

Variation: Add a splash of white wine to the herb mix for enhanced flavor.

98. AIR FRYER HERB-CRUSTED HADDOCK

Preparation Time: 10 minutes
Cooking Time: 15 minutes
Servings: 4

Ingredients:
- Haddock fillets: 4 (6 oz each)
- Fresh parsley: 2 tbsp, finely chopped
- Lemon zest: 1 tsp
- Olive oil: 1 tbsp
- Black pepper: 1/4 tsp

Directions:

Introduction: A light and flaky haddock with a crispy herb crust.

Cooking: Mix parsley, lemon zest, and black pepper. Brush fillets with olive oil, coat with the herb mixture. Cook in the Air Fryer at 350°F for 15 minutes.

Nutritional Information (per serving):
Calories: 190 kcal, Fat: 5g (0.18 oz), Carbs: 1g (0.04 oz), Protein: 35g (1.23 oz), Sodium: 100mg, Potassium: 450mg, Phosphorus: 250mg

Presentation: Serve with a lemon wedge and steamed asparagus.

Variation: Try using dill instead of parsley for a different flavor profile.

99. AIR FRYER SEABASS WITH GARLIC AND LIME

Preparation Time: 5 minutes
Cooking Time: 12 minutes
Servings: 4

Ingredients:
- Seabass fillets: 4 (6 oz each)
- Olive oil: 2 tbsp
- Garlic: 2 cloves, minced
- Lime: zest and juice of one
- Black pepper: 1/4 tsp

Directions:

Introduction: Delicately flavored seabass with a zesty lime and garlic topping.

Cooking: Combine olive oil, garlic, lime zest, and juice. Season fillets with pepper, brush with the lime mixture. Cook in the Air Fryer at 360°F for 12 minutes.

Nutritional Information (per serving):
Calories: 210 kcal, Fat: 8g (0.28 oz), Carbs: 2g (0.07 oz), Protein: 32g (1.13 oz), Sodium: 85mg, Potassium: 500mg, Phosphorus: 280mg

Presentation: Serve fillets with a side of wild rice.

Variation: Add chili flakes to the lime mixture for a spicy kick.

100. AIR FRYER PLAICE WITH CAPERS

Preparation Time: 5 minutes
Cooking Time: 10 minutes
Servings: 4

Ingredients:
- Plaice fillets: 4 (6 oz each)
- Olive oil: 2 tbsp
- Capers: 1 tbsp, rinsed and chopped
- Lemon juice: 1 tbsp
- Black pepper: 1/4 tsp

Directions:
Introduction: A simple yet flavorful plaice recipe with the tangy taste of capers.
Cooking: Brush plaice with olive oil and lemon juice. Sprinkle with capers and black pepper. Cook in the Air Fryer at 340°F for 10 minutes.

Nutritional Information (per serving):
Calories: 180 kcal, Fat: 7g (0.25 oz), Carbs: 1g (0.04 oz), Protein: 28g (0.99 oz), Sodium: 125mg, Potassium: 380mg, Phosphorus: 220mg

Presentation: Garnish with lemon slices and fresh parsley.

Variation: Substitute capers with chopped olives for a different briny flavor.

101. AIR FRYER SOLE IN PARCHMENT

Preparation Time: 10 minutes
Cooking Time: 12 minutes
Servings: 4

Ingredients:
- Sole fillets: 4 (6 oz each)
- Parchment paper
- Fresh herbs (parsley, thyme): 1 tbsp, chopped
- Butter: 1 tbsp, melted
- Lemon slices: 4
- Black pepper: 1/4 tsp

Directions:
Introduction: Sole cooked in parchment to seal in moisture and flavor.
Cooking: Place each fillet on a piece of parchment, top with herbs, a teaspoon of butter, and a lemon slice. Season with black pepper. Fold parchment to seal. Cook in the Air Fryer at 350°F for 12 minutes.

Nutritional Information (per serving):
Calories: 170 kcal, Fat: 6g (0.21 oz), Carbs: 1g (0.04 oz), Protein: 27g (0.95 oz), Sodium: 70mg, Potassium: 360mg, Phosphorus: 210mg

Presentation: Serve directly in the parchment for an elegant presentation.

Variation: Add thinly sliced vegetables like zucchini or carrots inside the parchment for extra flavor and nutrition.

102. AIR FRYER SALMON WITH DILL SAUCE

Preparation Time: 5 minutes
Cooking Time: 10 minutes
Servings: 4

Ingredients:
- Salmon fillets: 4 (6 oz each)
- Greek yogurt: 1/2 cup
- Dill: 2 tbsp, finely chopped
- Lemon juice: 2 tbsp

- Garlic powder: 1 tsp
- Olive oil: 1 tbsp
- Black pepper: 1/4 tsp

Directions:

Introduction: Salmon fillets served with a creamy dill sauce.

Cooking: Brush salmon with olive oil and season with black pepper. Cook in the Air Fryer at 400°F for 10 minutes. Mix yogurt, dill, lemon juice, and garlic powder to make the sauce.

Nutritional Information (per serving):
Calories: 290 kcal, Fat: 15g (0.53 oz), Carbs: 3g (0.11 oz), Protein: 35g (1.23 oz), Sodium: 90mg, Potassium: 520mg, Phosphorus: 300mg

Presentation: Serve the salmon topped with dill sauce and a side of steamed broccoli.

Variation: Add capers to the dill sauce for an extra tangy flavor.

103. AIR FRYER SCOTTISH KIPPERS WITH OAT CRUST

Preparation Time: 10 minutes
Cooking Time: 8 minutes
Servings: 4

Ingredients:
- Kippers (smoked herring fillets): 4 (4 oz each)
- Rolled oats: 1/4 cup, finely ground
- Lemon zest: 1 tsp
- Fresh thyme: 1 tbsp, chopped
- Olive oil: 1 tbsp
- Black pepper: 1/4 tsp

Directions:

Introduction: A Scottish-inspired dish, kippers with a crispy oat crust, made lighter and healthier in an Air Fryer.

Cooking: Mix ground oats, lemon zest, thyme, and black pepper in a bowl. Brush kippers with olive oil, then press the oat mixture onto the fillets. Cook in the Air Fryer at 360°F for 8 minutes, or until the oat crust is golden and crisp.

Nutritional Information (per serving):
Calories: 210 kcal, Fat: 12g (0.42 oz), Carbs: 6g (0.21 oz), Protein: 20g (0.71 oz), Sodium: 80mg, Potassium: 380mg, Phosphorus: 280mg

Presentation: Serve the kippers on a warm plate, accompanied by a fresh green salad and a wedge of lemon.

Variation: For a slight twist, add a pinch of smoked paprika to the oat mixture for extra smokiness and a subtle warmth.

104. AIR FRYER MACKEREL WITH HERB MARINADE

Preparation Time: 15 minutes (including marinating time)
Cooking Time: 10 minutes
Servings: 4

Ingredients:
- Mackerel fillets: 4 (6 oz each)
- Olive oil: 2 tbsp
- Lemon juice: 2 tbsp
- Fresh herbs (dill, parsley): 2 tbsp, chopped
- Garlic: 1 clove, minced
- Black pepper: 1/4 tsp

Directions:

Introduction: Flavor-packed mackerel fillets marinated in herbs and lemon, perfect for a quick and healthy meal.

Cooking: Combine olive oil, lemon juice, herbs, garlic, and black pepper in a bowl. Marinade mackerel fillets in the mixture for 10 minutes. Cook in the Air Fryer at 360°F for 10 minutes, turning halfway through.

Nutritional Information (per serving):
Calories: 290 kcal, Fat: 22g (0.78 oz), Carbs: 1g (0.04 oz), Protein: 22g (0.78 oz), Sodium: 85mg, Potassium: 500mg, Phosphorus: 280mg

Presentation: Plate the mackerel with a fresh herb garnish and a side of roasted cherry tomatoes.

Variation: Add a sprinkle of crushed red pepper to the marinade for a spicy version.

VEGETARIAN DISJES

105. AIR FRYER STUFFED MUSHROOMS

Preparation Time: 10 minutes
Cooking Time: 8 minutes
Servings: 4

Ingredients:
- Large mushrooms: 8 (such as Portobello)
- Ricotta cheese: 1/2 cup
- Spinach: 1 cup, chopped
- Garlic: 2 cloves, minced
- Olive oil: 1 tbsp
- Black pepper: 1/4 tsp

Directions:
Remove stems from mushrooms, chop the stems and mix with ricotta, spinach, and garlic. Stuff the mixture back into the mushroom caps, drizzle with olive oil, and season with black pepper. Cook in the Air Fryer at 360°F for 8 minutes.

Nutritional Information (per serving):
Calories: 120 kcal, Fat: 7g (0.25 oz), Carbs: 8g (0.28 oz), Protein: 6g (0.21 oz), Sodium: 60mg, Potassium: 300mg, Phosphorus: 100mg

Presentation: Garnish with chopped parsley.

Variation: Add chopped walnuts for a crunchy texture.

106. AIR FRYER SWEET POTATO CAKES

Preparation Time: 15 minutes
Cooking Time: 10 minutes
Servings: 4

Ingredients:
- Sweet potatoes: 2, peeled and grated
- Scallions: 2, finely chopped
- Flour: 1/4 cup
- Egg: 1, beaten
- Olive oil: 1 tbsp
- Black pepper: 1/4 tsp

Directions:
Mix all ingredients in a bowl. Form into patties. Brush with olive oil and cook in the Air Fryer at 380°F for 10 minutes, flipping halfway through.

Nutritional Information (per serving):
Calories: 200 kcal, Fat: 7g (0.25 oz), Carbs: 30g (1.06 oz), Protein: 4g (0.14 oz), Sodium: 75mg, Potassium: 450mg, Phosphorus: 90mg

Presentation: Serve with a dollop of low-fat yogurt.

Variation: Add a pinch of curry powder for extra flavor.

107. AIR FRYER CHEESY CAULIFLOWER

Preparation Time: 5 minutes
Cooking Time: 15 minutes
Servings: 4

Ingredients:
- Cauliflower: 1 head, cut into florets
- Low-sodium cheddar cheese: 1/2 cup, grated
- Paprika: 1 tsp
- Olive oil: 1 tbsp
- Black pepper: 1/4 tsp

Directions:
Toss cauliflower with olive oil, paprika, and black pepper. Halfway through cooking at 360°F for 15 minutes, sprinkle with cheese and continue to cook until golden.

Nutritional Information (per serving):
Calories: 150 kcal, Fat: 9g (0.32 oz), Carbs: 10g (0.35 oz), Protein: 7g (0.25 oz), Sodium: 80mg, Potassium: 300mg, Phosphorus: 150mg

Presentation: Garnish with chopped chives.
Variation: Add garlic powder for a garlic cheese version.

108. AIR FRYER BUTTERNUT SQUASH FRIES

Preparation Time: 10 minutes
Cooking Time: 15 minutes
Servings: 4

Ingredients:
- Butternut squash: 1, peeled and cut into fries
- Olive oil: 2 tbsp
- Thyme: 1 tsp, dried
- Black pepper: 1/4 tsp

Directions:
Toss butternut squash fries with olive oil, thyme, and black pepper. Cook in the Air Fryer at 380°F for 15 minutes, shaking occasionally, until crispy.

Nutritional Information (per serving):
Calories: 110 kcal, Fat: 7g (0.25 oz), Carbs: 12g (0.42 oz), Protein: 1g (0.04 oz), Sodium: 5mg, Potassium: 350mg, Phosphorus: 40mg

Presentation: Serve with a side of low-sodium ketchup.
Variation: Sprinkle with cinnamon instead of thyme for a sweet version.

109. AIR FRYER BRUSSELS SPROUTS WITH BALSAMIC

Preparation Time: 5 minutes
Cooking Time: 12 minutes
Servings: 4

Ingredients:
- Brussels sprouts: 1 lb, halved
- Olive oil: 1 tbsp
- Balsamic vinegar: 2 tbsp
- Black pepper: 1/4 tsp

Directions:

Toss Brussels sprouts with olive oil, balsamic vinegar, and black pepper. Cook in the Air Fryer at 400°F for 12 minutes, until caramelized and tender.

Nutritional Information (per serving):
Calories: 90 kcal, Fat: 4g (0.14 oz), Carbs: 10g (0.35 oz), Protein: 4g (0.14 oz), Sodium: 25mg, Potassium: 350mg, Phosphorus: 60mg

Presentation: Garnish with a sprinkle of grated Parmesan (optional).

Variation: Add a spoonful of honey with the balsamic for a sweet and tangy flavor.

110. AIR FRYER BEETROOT CHIPS

Preparation Time: 10 minutes
Cooking Time: 15 minutes
Servings: 4

Ingredients:
- Beetroots: 3, peeled and thinly sliced
- Olive oil: 1 tbsp
- Sea salt: a pinch (optional, ensure low sodium intake)
- Black pepper: 1/4 tsp

Directions:
Toss beetroot slices with olive oil and black pepper. Cook in the Air Fryer at 360°F for 15 minutes, turning halfway through, until crispy.

Nutritional Information (per serving):
Calories: 70 kcal, Fat: 3.5g (0.12 oz), Carbs: 9g (0.32 oz), Protein: 2g (0.07 oz), Sodium: 40mg, Potassium: 300mg, Phosphorus: 50mg

Presentation: Serve these vibrant chips as a snack or side.

Variation: Dust with dried rosemary before cooking for an aromatic twist.

111. AIR FRYER GARLIC HERB ZUCCHINI

Preparation Time: 5 minutes
Cooking Time: 10 minutes
Servings: 4

Ingredients:
- Zucchini: 2, sliced into rounds
- Olive oil: 1 tbsp
- Garlic powder: 1 tsp
- Dried herbs (basil, oregano): 1 tsp
- Black pepper: 1/4 tsp

Directions:
Toss zucchini slices with olive oil, garlic powder, herbs, and black pepper. Cook in the Air Fryer at 380°F for 10 minutes, until tender and golden.

Nutritional Information (per serving):
Calories: 60 kcal, Fat: 3.5g (0.12 oz), Carbs: 6g (0.21 oz), Protein: 2g (0.07 oz), Sodium: 10mg, Potassium: 290mg, Phosphorus: 50mg

Presentation: Serve as a healthy side dish or add to salads.

Variation: Sprinkle with Parmesan cheese in the last 2 minutes of cooking for a cheesy finish.

112. AIR FRYER STUFFED BELL PEPPERS

Preparation Time: 15 minutes
Cooking Time: 10 minutes
Servings: 4

Ingredients:
- Bell peppers: 4, tops cut off and seeded
- Cooked quinoa: 1 cup
- Cooked black beans: 1/2 cup
- Corn: 1/2 cup
- Chopped cilantro: 2 tbsp
- Olive oil: 1 tbsp
- Black pepper: 1/4 tsp

Directions:
Mix quinoa, black beans, corn, and cilantro with a drizzle of olive oil and black pepper. Stuff this mixture into the bell peppers. Cook in the Air Fryer at 360°F for 10 minutes.

Nutritional Information (per serving):
Calories: 200 kcal, Fat: 5g (0.18 oz), Carbs: 30g (1.06 oz), Protein: 8g (0.28 oz), Sodium: 10mg, Potassium: 450mg, Phosphorus: 100mg

Presentation: Serve as a main dish or hearty side.

Variation: Add a sprinkle of low-sodium cheese before cooking for a melty top.

113. AIR FRYER ASPARAGUS SPEARS

Preparation Time: 5 minutes
Cooking Time: 8 minutes
Servings: 4

Ingredients:
- Asparagus: 1 lb, trimmed
- Olive oil: 1 tbsp
- Lemon zest: 1 tsp
- Black pepper: 1/4 tsp

Directions:
Toss asparagus with olive oil, lemon zest, and black pepper. Cook in the Air Fryer at 400°F for 8 minutes or until tender and slightly crispy.

Nutritional Information (per serving):
Calories: 50 kcal, Fat: 3.5g (0.12 oz), Carbs: 4g (0.14 oz), Protein: 3g (0.11 oz), Sodium: 2mg, Potassium: 230mg, Phosphorus: 55mg

Presentation: Perfect as a side dish, garnish with additional lemon zest.

Variation: Sprinkle with finely grated Parmesan in the last minute of cooking for a cheesy crust.

114. AIR FRYER TOMATO AND BASIL BRUSCHETTA

Preparation Time: 10 minutes
Cooking Time: 5 minutes
Servings: 4

Ingredients:
- Ciabatta bread: 1 loaf, sliced
- Cherry tomatoes: 1 cup, halved
- Fresh basil: 1/4 cup, chopped
- Olive oil: 2 tbsp
- Garlic: 1 clove, minced
- Black pepper: 1/4 tsp

Directions:
Toss tomatoes with basil, garlic, and olive oil. Season with black pepper. Top ciabatta slices with the tomato mixture. Cook in the Air Fryer at 360°F for 5 minutes, until the bread is crispy.

Nutritional Information (per serving):
Calories: 180 kcal, Fat: 7g (0.25 oz), Carbs: 24g (0.85 oz), Protein: 5g (0.18 oz), Sodium: 180mg, Potassium: 150mg, Phosphorus: 70mg

Presentation: Serve as an appetizer or a light meal.

Variation: Drizzle with balsamic glaze before serving for added sweetness and tang.

Chapter 4. Vegetable side dishes, salads

VEGETABLE SIDE DISHES

115. ROASTED PARSNIPS WITH THYME

Preparation Time: 10 minutes
Cooking Time: 25 minutes
Servings: 4

Ingredients:
- Parsnips: 1 lb, peeled and sliced
- Olive oil: 1 tbsp
- Thyme: 1 tsp, dried
- Black pepper: 1/4 tsp

Directions:
Toss parsnips with olive oil, thyme, and black pepper. Roast in an Air Fryer at 400°F for 25 minutes or until golden and tender.

Nutritional Information (per serving):
Calories: 120 kcal, Fat: 3.5g (0.12 oz), Carbs: 22g (0.77 oz), Protein: 2g (0.07 oz), Sodium: 10mg, Potassium: 375mg, Phosphorus: 75mg

Presentation: Serve garnished with fresh thyme sprigs.

Variation: For a sweeter version, drizzle with a little honey before serving.

Storage: Best eaten fresh, but leftovers can be refrigerated for up to 2 days.

116. BUTTERED PEAS WITH MINT

Preparation Time: 5 minutes
Cooking Time: 10 minutes
Servings: 4

Ingredients:
- Peas: 2 cups, frozen
- Butter: 1 tbsp (low sodium)
- Mint: 2 tbsp, chopped
- Black pepper: 1/8 tsp

Directions:
Cook peas according to package instructions, then stir in butter, chopped mint, and black pepper.

Nutritional Information (per serving):
Calories: 90 kcal, Fat: 3g (0.11 oz), Carbs: 13g (0.46 oz), Protein: 4g (0.14 oz), Sodium: 25mg, Potassium: 210mg, Phosphorus: 60mg

Presentation: Serve in a small bowl or as a side dish to the main course.

Variation: Use olive oil instead of butter for a vegan option.

Storage: Refrigerate in an airtight container for up to 3 days.

117. SCOTTISH NEEPS AND TATTIES

Preparation Time: 15 minutes
Cooking Time: 20 minutes
Servings: 4

Ingredients:
- Swede (rutabaga): 1 lb, peeled and cubed
- Potatoes: 1 lb, peeled and cubed
- Butter: 1 tbsp (low sodium)
- Black pepper: 1/4 tsp

Directions:
Boil swede and potatoes until tender, about 20 minutes. Mash with butter and season with black pepper.

Nutritional Information (per serving):
Calories: 180 kcal, Fat: 3g (0.11 oz), Carbs: 34g (1.20 oz), Protein: 4g (0.14 oz), Sodium: 30mg, Potassium: 600mg, Phosphorus: 90mg

Presentation: Serve heaped on a plate, perhaps with a sprinkle of chives.

Variation: Add a pinch of nutmeg for additional warmth and flavor.

Storage: Can be stored in the refrigerator for up to 3 days.

118. BRAISED RED CABBAGE

Preparation Time: 10 minutes
Cooking Time: 60 minutes
Servings: 4

Ingredients:
- Red cabbage: 1 medium head, shredded
- Apples: 2, peeled and sliced
- Vinegar: 2 tbsp (apple cider vinegar)
- Water: 1/2 cup
- Cinnamon: 1 tsp

Directions:
Combine all ingredients in a large pot. Cover and simmer for about 60 minutes, stirring occasionally, until cabbage is tender and sweet.

Nutritional Information (per serving):
Calories: 100 kcal, Fat: 0.5g (0.02 oz), Carbs: 25g (0.88 oz), Protein: 2g (0.07 oz), Sodium: 20mg, Potassium: 290mg, Phosphorus: 50mg

Presentation: Serve hot, with a garnish of apple slices.

Variation: For added sweetness, stir in a spoonful of honey or brown sugar towards the end of cooking.

Storage: Refrigerate for up to 4 days or freeze for up to a month.

119. GRILLED LEEKS WITH VINAIGRETTE

Preparation Time: 10 minutes
Cooking Time: 15 minutes
Servings: 4

Ingredients:
- Leeks: 4, trimmed and halved lengthwise
- Olive oil: 2 tbsp
- Lemon juice: 1 tbsp
- Dijon mustard: 1 tsp (low sodium)
- Black pepper: 1/4 tsp

Directions:
Brush leeks with olive oil and grill in the Air Fryer at 375°F for 15 minutes. Whisk together lemon juice, mustard, and black pepper to make a vinaigrette. Drizzle over cooked leeks.

Nutritional Information (per serving):

Calories: 110 kcal, **Fat:** 7g (0.25 oz), **Carbs:** 10g (0.35 oz), **Protein:** 1g (0.04 oz), **Sodium:** 30mg, **Potassium:** 120mg, **Phosphorus:** 35mg

Presentation: Arrange on a platter and drizzle with vinaigrette.

Variation: Add chopped fresh herbs such as parsley or tarragon to the vinaigrette for more flavor.

Storage: Best enjoyed fresh, but can be refrigerated for up to 2 days.

120. CELERIAC MASH

Preparation Time: 10 minutes
Cooking Time: 20 minutes
Servings: 4

Ingredients:
- Celeriac: 1 lb, peeled and cubed
- Low-fat milk: 1/4 cup
- Butter: 1 tbsp (unsalted)
- Black pepper: 1/4 tsp

Directions:
Boil celeriac until tender, about 20 minutes. Drain and mash with milk and butter until smooth. Season with black pepper.

Nutritional Information (per serving):
Calories: 120 kcal, Fat: 5g (0.18 oz), Carbs: 17g (0.60 oz), Protein: 2g (0.07 oz), Sodium: 40mg, Potassium: 300mg, Phosphorus: 70mg

Storage: Refrigerate in an airtight container for up to 3 days.

Presentation: Serve warm, garnished with fresh parsley if desired.

Variations: Substitute olive oil for butter for a vegan option.

121. ROASTED SWEDE WITH ROSEMARY

Preparation Time: 10 minutes
Cooking Time: 35 minutes
Servings: 4

Ingredients:
- Swede (rutabaga): 1 lb, peeled and diced
- Olive oil: 1 tbsp
- Rosemary: 1 tsp, chopped
- Black pepper: 1/4 tsp

Directions:
Toss swede with olive oil, rosemary, and black pepper. Roast in an oven preheated to 400°F for 35 minutes or until tender and golden.

Nutritional Information (per serving):
Calories: 90 kcal, Fat: 3.5g (0.12 oz), Carbs: 14g (0.49 oz), Protein: 2g (0.07 oz), Sodium: 20mg, Potassium: 350mg, Phosphorus: 60mg

Storage: Refrigerate leftovers for up to 2 days in a sealed container.

Presentation: Serve as a side dish, perhaps alongside a main course of grilled fish or chicken.

Variations: Add a sprinkle of garlic powder for extra flavor.

122. BUTTERED KALE WITH NUTMEG

Preparation Time: 5 minutes
Cooking Time: 10 minutes
Servings: 4

Ingredients:

- Kale: 1 lb, stems removed and leaves chopped
- Butter: 2 tbsp (unsalted)
- Nutmeg: 1/4 tsp, grated
- Black pepper: 1/8 tsp

Directions:
Steam kale until wilted, about 5 minutes. Toss with butter, nutmeg, and black pepper while still warm.

Nutritional Information (per serving): Calories: 110 kcal, Fat: 6g (0.21 oz), Carbs: 12g (0.42 oz), Protein: 4g (0.14 oz), Sodium: 30mg, Potassium: 480mg, Phosphorus: 50mg

Storage: Best enjoyed fresh, but can be stored in the refrigerator for up to 1 day.

Presentation: Serve immediately, ideal as a comforting winter side.

Variations: For a vegan alternative, use olive oil instead of butter.

123. MINTED PEAS AND CARROTS

Preparation Time: 5 minutes
Cooking Time: 8 minutes
Servings: 4

Ingredients:
- Peas: 1 cup, fresh or frozen
- Carrots: 1 cup, diced
- Mint: 2 tbsp, chopped
- Butter: 1 tbsp (unsalted)
- Black pepper: 1/4 tsp

Directions:
Boil carrots and peas until tender, about 8 minutes. Drain and toss with butter, mint, and black pepper.

Nutritional Information (per serving): Calories: 80 kcal, Fat: 3g (0.11 oz), Carbs: 12g (0.42 oz), Protein: 2g (0.07 oz), Sodium: 25mg, Potassium: 240mg, Phosphorus: 45mg

Storage: Refrigerate in an airtight container for up to 2 days.

Presentation: Serve hot, perfect as a colorful addition to any plate.

Variations: Sprinkle with lemon zest for added freshness.

124. BALSAMIC GLAZED BRUSSELS SPROUTS

Preparation Time: 10 minutes
Cooking Time: 20 minutes
Servings: 4

Ingredients:
- Brussels sprouts: 1 lb, trimmed and halved
- Olive oil: 2 tbsp
- Balsamic vinegar: 2 tbsp
- Black pepper: 1/4 tsp

Directions:
Toss Brussels sprouts with olive oil and black pepper. Roast in an oven preheated to 400°F for 20 minutes. Drizzle with balsamic vinegar and return to the oven for 5 more minutes.

Nutritional Information (per serving): Calories: 90 kcal, Fat: 7g (0.25 oz), Carbs: 6g (0.21 oz), Protein: 2g (0.07 oz), Sodium: 20mg, Potassium: 250mg, Phosphorus: 50mg

Storage: Best enjoyed fresh, but can be refrigerated for up to 2 days.

Presentation: Serve warm, garnished with a sprinkle of fresh thyme.

Variations: Add a handful of chopped walnuts for extra crunch.

VEGETABLE SALADS

125. BEETROOT AND ORANGE SALAD

Preparation Time: 15 minutes
Cooking Time: 0 minutes
Servings: 4

Ingredients:
- Cooked beetroot, thinly sliced: 4 (approx. 1 lb / 450g)
- Oranges, peeled and segmented: 2 (300g / 10.5 oz)
- Red onion, thinly sliced: 1/2 (50g / 1.75 oz)
- Extra virgin olive oil: 2 tbsp (30ml / 1 oz)
- Fresh mint leaves: 2 tbsp (6g / 0.21 oz)
- Black pepper: 1/4 tsp (0.5g / 0.02 oz)

Directions:
Arrange the beetroot slices on a serving platter.
Scatter the orange segments and red onion slices over the beetroot.
Drizzle with olive oil and sprinkle with black pepper.
Garnish with fresh mint leaves.

Nutritional Information (per serving):
Calories: 110 kcal, Fat: 5g (0.18 oz), Carbs: 13g (0.46 oz), Protein: 2g (0.07 oz), Sodium: 30mg, Potassium: 270mg, Phosphorus: 40mg

Storage: Store leftovers in an airtight container in the refrigerator for up to 2 days.

Presentation: Serve on a large platter with a garnish of fresh mint.

Variations: Add a few toasted pine nuts for extra texture and flavor.

126. WATERCRESS AND PEAR SALAD

Preparation Time: 10 minutes
Cooking Time: 0 minutes
Servings: 4

Ingredients:
- Fresh watercress: 4 cups (120g / 4.2 oz)
- Pears, thinly sliced: 2 (300g / 10.5 oz)
- Lemon juice: 1 tbsp (15ml / 0.5 oz)
- Extra virgin olive oil: 2 tbsp (30ml / 1 oz)
- Black pepper: 1/4 tsp (0.5g / 0.02 oz)

Directions:
Toss the watercress and pear slices in a large bowl.
Drizzle with lemon juice and olive oil.
Season with black pepper and toss again.

Nutritional Information (per serving):
Calories: 90 kcal, Fat: 5g (0.18 oz), Carbs: 11g (0.39 oz), Protein: 2g (0.07 oz), Sodium: 10mg, Potassium: 230mg, Phosphorus: 30mg

Storage: Best enjoyed fresh. Store leftovers in an airtight container in the refrigerator for up to 1 day.

Presentation: Serve in a large bowl with lemon wedges on the side.

Variations: Add thin slices of radish for extra crunch and color.

127. RADISH AND CUCUMBER SALAD

Preparation Time: 10 minutes
Cooking Time: 0 minutes

Servings: 4

Ingredients:
- Radishes, thinly sliced: 1 cup (100g / 3.5 oz)
- Cucumber, thinly sliced: 1 (200g / 7 oz)
- Fresh dill, chopped: 1 tbsp (1.5g / 0.05 oz)
- Greek yogurt: 2 tbsp (30ml / 1 oz)
- Lemon juice: 1 tbsp (15ml / 0.5 oz)
- Black pepper: 1/4 tsp (0.5g / 0.02 oz)

Directions:
1. In a bowl, combine the radishes, cucumber, and dill.
In a separate small bowl, mix the Greek yogurt and lemon juice.
3. Drizzle the yogurt dressing over the salad and toss to combine.
4. Season with black pepper.

Nutritional Information (per serving):
Calories: 50 kcal, Fat: 2g (0.07 oz), Carbs: 7g (0.25 oz), Protein: 2g (0.07 oz), Sodium: 30mg, Potassium: 170mg, Phosphorus: 30mg

Storage: Store leftovers in an airtight container in the refrigerator for up to 1 day.

Presentation: Serve in small bowls, garnished with extra dill.

Variations: Use low-fat yogurt for a lighter version.

128. ROASTED VEGETABLE SALAD

Preparation Time: 15 minutes
Cooking Time: 30 minutes
Servings: 4

Ingredients:
- Carrots, chopped: 2 (200g / 7 oz)
- Bell peppers, chopped: 2 (300g / 10.5 oz)
- Zucchini, chopped: 1 (200g / 7 oz)
- Red onion, chopped: 1 (100g / 3.5 oz)
- Extra virgin olive oil: 2 tbsp (30ml / 1 oz)
- Fresh thyme: 1 tbsp (1.5g / 0.05 oz)
- Black pepper: 1/4 tsp (0.5g / 0.02 oz)

Directions:
1. Preheat the oven to 400°F (200°C).
Toss the chopped vegetables with olive oil, thyme, and black pepper.
3. Spread the vegetables on a baking sheet and roast for 30 minutes, until tender and slightly caramelized.
4. Allow to cool slightly before serving.

Nutritional Information (per serving):
Calories: 120 kcal, Fat: 7g (0.25 oz), Carbs: 12g (0.42 oz), Protein: 2g (0.07 oz), Sodium: 20mg, Potassium: 350mg, Phosphorus: 40mg

Storage: Store leftovers in an airtight container in the refrigerator for up to 2 days.

Presentation: Serve on a large platter, garnished with fresh thyme.

Variations: Add a squeeze of lemon juice before serving for extra freshness.

129. PEA AND MINT SALAD

Preparation Time: 10 minutes
Cooking Time: 5 minutes
Servings: 4

Ingredients:
- Fresh or frozen peas: 2 cups (300g / 10.5 oz)
- Fresh mint leaves, chopped: 2 tbsp (6g / 0.21 oz)
- Extra virgin olive oil: 1 tbsp (15ml / 0.5 oz)

- Lemon juice: 1 tbsp (15ml / 0.5 oz)
- Black pepper: 1/4 tsp (0.5g / 0.02 oz)

Directions:

1. If using fresh peas, blanch them in boiling water for 2-3 minutes, then drain and cool. If using frozen peas, thaw and drain.
In a bowl, combine the peas, chopped mint, olive oil, and lemon juice.
3. Toss to combine and season with black pepper.

Nutritional Information (per serving):
Calories: 70 kcal, Fat: 3g (0.11 oz), Carbs: 10g (0.35 oz), Protein: 3g (0.11 oz), Sodium: 20mg, Potassium: 150mg, Phosphorus: 40mg

Storage: Store leftovers in an airtight container in the refrigerator for up to 1 day.

Presentation: Serve in a bowl garnished with whole mint leaves.

Variations: Add a small amount of finely chopped red onion for extra flavor.

130. CABBAGE AND APPLE SALAD

Preparation Time: 15 minutes
Cooking Time: 0 minutes
Servings: 4

Ingredients:
- Green cabbage, thinly sliced: 3 cups (300g / 10.5 oz)
- Apples, thinly sliced: 2 (300g / 10.5 oz)
- Fresh lemon juice: 2 tbsp (30ml / 1 oz)
- Extra virgin olive oil: 1 tbsp (15ml / 0.5 oz)
- Fresh parsley, chopped: 2 tbsp (6g / 0.21 oz)
- Black pepper: 1/4 tsp (0.5g / 0.02 oz)

Directions:

1. In a large bowl, combine the cabbage and apple slices.
In a small bowl, whisk together the lemon juice and olive oil.
3. Pour the dressing over the cabbage and apple mixture.
4. Toss to combine and season with black pepper.
5. Garnish with chopped parsley.

Nutritional Information (per serving):
Calories: 80 kcal, Fat: 3g (0.11 oz), Carbs: 12g (0.42 oz), Protein: 1g (0.04 oz), Sodium: 15mg, Potassium: 180mg, Phosphorus: 20mg

Storage: Store leftovers in an airtight container in the refrigerator for up to 1 day.

Presentation: Serve in a large bowl with parsley sprinkled on top.

Variations: Add a handful of raisins for a touch of sweetness.

131. CARROT AND CORIANDER SALAD

Preparation Time: 10 minutes
Cooking Time: 0 minutes
Servings: 4

Ingredients:
- Carrots, grated: 3 (300g / 10.5 oz)
- Fresh coriander leaves, chopped: 2 tbsp (6g / 0.21 oz)
- Lemon juice: 2 tbsp (30ml / 1 oz)
- Extra virgin olive oil: 1 tbsp (15ml / 0.5 oz)
- Black pepper: 1/4 tsp (0.5g / 0.02 oz)

Directions:

1. In a bowl, combine the grated carrots and chopped coriander.

In a small bowl, whisk together the lemon juice and olive oil.

3. Pour the dressing over the carrot mixture.

4. Toss to combine and season with black pepper.

Nutritional Information (per serving):
Calories: 60 kcal, Fat: 3g (0.11 oz), Carbs: 8g (0.28 oz), Protein: 1g (0.04 oz), Sodium: 15mg, Potassium: 220mg, Phosphorus: 25mg

Storage: Store leftovers in an airtight container in the refrigerator for up to 1 day.

Presentation: Serve in a bowl, garnished with additional coriander leaves.

Variations: Add a sprinkle of toasted sesame seeds for extra texture.

132. SPRING GREENS SALAD

Preparation Time: 10 minutes
Cooking Time: 0 minutes
Servings: 4

Ingredients:
- Mixed spring greens (spinach, arugula, etc.): 4 cups (120g / 4.2 oz)
- Cherry tomatoes, halved: 1 cup (150g / 5.3 oz)
- Radishes, thinly sliced: 1/2 cup (50g / 1.75 oz)
- Cucumber, thinly sliced: 1/2 cup (50g / 1.75 oz)
- Balsamic vinegar: 2 tbsp (30ml / 1 oz)
- Extra virgin olive oil: 1 tbsp (15ml / 0.5 oz)
- Black pepper: 1/4 tsp (0.5g / 0.02 oz)

Directions:
1. In a large bowl, combine the mixed greens, cherry tomatoes, radishes, and cucumber.

In a small bowl, whisk together the balsamic vinegar and olive oil.

3. Pour the dressing over the salad and toss to combine.

4. Season with black pepper.

Nutritional Information (per serving):
Calories: 50 kcal, Fat: 3g (0.11 oz), Carbs: 6g (0.21 oz), Protein: 1g (0.04 oz), Sodium: 10mg, Potassium: 150mg, Phosphorus: 20mg

Storage: Best enjoyed fresh. Store leftovers in an airtight container in the refrigerator for up to 1 day.

Presentation: Serve in a large bowl with a sprinkle of black pepper on top.

Variations: Add a handful of sunflower seeds for a crunchy texture.

133. TOMATO AND BASIL SALAD

Preparation Time: 10 minutes
Cooking Time: 0 minutes
Servings: 4

Ingredients:
- Ripe tomatoes, sliced: 4 (400g / 14 oz)
- Fresh basil leaves: 1/4 cup (10g / 0.35 oz)
- Extra virgin olive oil: 2 tbsp (30ml / 1 oz)
- Balsamic vinegar: 1 tbsp (15ml / 0.5 oz)
- Black pepper: 1/4 tsp (0.5g / 0.02 oz)

Directions:
1. Arrange the tomato slices on a serving platter.

Tear the basil leaves and scatter them over the tomatoes.

3. Drizzle with olive oil and balsamic vinegar.

4. Season with black pepper.

Nutritional Information (per serving):
Calories: 60 kcal, Fat: 4g (0.14 oz), Carbs: 5g (0.18 oz), Protein: 1g (0.04 oz), Sodium: 10mg, Potassium: 250mg, Phosphorus: 20mg

Storage: Best enjoyed fresh. Store leftovers in an airtight container in the refrigerator for up to 1 day.

Presentation: Serve on a platter, garnished with whole basil leaves.

Variations: Add a few slices of mozzarella for a Caprese-style salad.

134. ASPARAGUS AND LEMON SALAD

Preparation Time: 10 minutes
Cooking Time: 5 minutes
Servings: 4

Ingredients:
- Fresh asparagus, trimmed: 1 lb (450g)
- Lemon zest: 1 tsp (2g / 0.07 oz)
- Lemon juice: 2 tbsp (30ml / 1 oz)
- Extra virgin olive oil: 1 tbsp (15ml / 0.5 oz)
- Fresh parsley, chopped: 1 tbsp (3g / 0.1 oz)
- Black pepper: 1/4 tsp (0.5g / 0.02 oz)

Directions:
1. Blanch the asparagus in boiling water for 2-3 minutes, then drain and cool under cold water.
In a bowl, combine the blanched asparagus, lemon zest, lemon juice, and olive oil.
3. Toss to combine and season with black pepper.
4. Garnish with chopped parsley.

Nutritional Information (per serving):
Calories: 60 kcal, Fat: 4g (0.14 oz), Carbs: 5g (0.18 oz), Protein: 2g (0.07 oz), Sodium: 10mg, Potassium: 180mg, Phosphorus: 30mg

Storage: Store leftovers in an airtight container in the refrigerator for up to 2 days.

Presentation: Serve on a platter with a sprinkle of lemon zest on top.

Variations: Add a few shavings of Parmesan cheese for extra flavor.

Chapter 5: Hot & Cold Starters

HOT STARTERS

GRILLED STARTERS

135. GRILLED AUBERGINE ROLLS

Preparation Time: 15 minutes
Cooking Time: 10 minutes
Servings: 4

Ingredients:
- Aubergine, thinly sliced lengthwise: 1 large (300g / 10.5 oz)
- Low-fat ricotta cheese: 1 cup (240g / 8.5 oz)
- Fresh basil leaves, chopped: 2 tbsp (6g / 0.21 oz)
- Garlic, minced: 1 clove (3g / 0.11 oz)
- Black pepper: 1/4 tsp (0.5g / 0.02 oz)
- Extra virgin olive oil: 2 tbsp (30ml / 1 oz)

Directions:
Preheat the grill to medium-high heat.
Brush the aubergine slices with olive oil and grill for 3-4 minutes on each side, until tender.
In a bowl, mix the ricotta cheese, basil, garlic, and black pepper.
Place a spoonful of the cheese mixture on each aubergine slice and roll up.
Serve warm with a drizzle of olive oil.

Nutritional Information (per serving):
Calories: 120 kcal, Fat: 7g (0.25 oz), Carbs: 10g (0.35 oz), Protein: 4g (0.14 oz), Sodium: 40mg, Potassium: 280mg, Phosphorus: 80mg

Storage: Best enjoyed fresh. Store leftovers in an airtight container in the refrigerator for up to 1 day.

Presentation: Arrange the rolls on a platter and garnish with fresh basil leaves.

Variations: Use goat cheese instead of ricotta for a different flavor.

136. GRILLED COURGETTE AND PEPPER SKEWERS

Preparation Time: 15 minutes
Cooking Time: 10 minutes
Servings: 4

Ingredients:
- Courgettes, cut into thick slices: 2 (300g / 10.5 oz)
- Bell peppers, cut into chunks: 2 (300g / 10.5 oz)
- Fresh rosemary, chopped: 1 tbsp (1.5g / 0.05 oz)
- Extra virgin olive oil: 2 tbsp (30ml / 1 oz)
- Black pepper: 1/4 tsp (0.5g / 0.02 oz)

Directions:
Preheat the grill to medium-high heat.
Thread the courgette and pepper chunks onto skewers.
In a bowl, mix the olive oil, rosemary, and black pepper.
Brush the skewers with the olive oil mixture.

Grill for 8-10 minutes, turning occasionally, until the vegetables are tender and lightly charred.

Nutritional Information (per serving):
Calories: 90 kcal, Fat: 5g (0.18 oz), Carbs: 10g (0.35 oz), Protein: 2g (0.07 oz), Sodium: 15mg, Potassium: 300mg, Phosphorus: 40mg

Storage: Best enjoyed fresh. Store leftovers in an airtight container in the refrigerator for up to 1 day.

Presentation: Serve the skewers on a platter with a sprinkle of fresh rosemary.

Variations: Add cherry tomatoes to the skewers for extra color and flavor.

137. GRILLED ASPARAGUS WITH LEMON ZEST

Preparation Time: 10 minutes
Cooking Time: 8 minutes
Servings: 4

Ingredients:
- Fresh asparagus, trimmed: 1 lb (450g)
- Extra virgin olive oil: 2 tbsp (30ml / 1 oz)
- Lemon zest: 1 tsp (2g / 0.07 oz)
- Black pepper: 1/4 tsp (0.5g / 0.02 oz)

Directions:
Preheat the grill to medium-high heat.
Toss the asparagus with olive oil and black pepper.
Grill for 6-8 minutes, turning occasionally, until tender and lightly charred.
Transfer to a serving platter and sprinkle with lemon zest.

Nutritional Information (per serving):
Calories: 70 kcal, Fat: 4g (0.14 oz), Carbs: 7g (0.25 oz), Protein: 3g (0.11 oz), Sodium: 10mg, Potassium: 180mg, Phosphorus: 30mg

Storage: Best enjoyed fresh. Store leftovers in an airtight container in the refrigerator for up to 2 days.

Presentation: Serve on a platter with lemon wedges.

Variations: Add a drizzle of balsamic glaze before serving.

138. GRILLED PORTOBELLO MUSHROOMS

Preparation Time: 10 minutes
Cooking Time: 10 minutes
Servings: 4

Ingredients:
- Portobello mushrooms, stems removed: 4 large (400g / 14 oz)
- Balsamic vinegar: 2 tbsp (30ml / 1 oz)
- Extra virgin olive oil: 2 tbsp (30ml / 1 oz)
- Fresh thyme, chopped: 1 tbsp (1.5g / 0.05 oz)
- Black pepper: 1/4 tsp (0.5g / 0.02 oz)

Directions:
Preheat the grill to medium-high heat.
In a bowl, mix the balsamic vinegar, olive oil, thyme, and black pepper.
Brush the mushrooms with the balsamic mixture.
Grill the mushrooms for 5 minutes on each side, until tender.

Nutritional Information (per serving):
Calories: 80 kcal, Fat: 6g (0.21 oz), Carbs: 6g (0.21

oz), Protein: 2g (0.07 oz), Sodium: 10mg, Potassium: 250mg, Phosphorus: 50mg

Storage: Best enjoyed fresh. Store leftovers in an airtight container in the refrigerator for up to 1 day.

Presentation: Serve on a platter garnished with fresh thyme.

Variations: Add a sprinkle of grated Parmesan cheese before serving.

SOUP STARTERS

139. LEEK AND POTATO SOUP

Preparation Time: 15 minutes
Cooking Time: 30 minutes
Servings: 6

Ingredients:
- Leeks, chopped: 3 (300g / 10.5 oz)
- Potatoes, peeled and diced: 2 cups (300g / 10.5 oz)
- Low-sodium vegetable broth: 4 cups (1 litre / 34 fl oz)
- Black pepper: 1/4 tsp (0.5g / 0.02 oz)
- Extra virgin olive oil: 2 tbsp (30ml / 1 oz)
- Fresh parsley, chopped: 2 tbsp (6g / 0.21 oz)

Directions:
Heat the olive oil in a large pot over medium heat. Add the leeks and cook until softened, about 5 minutes.
Add the potatoes and vegetable broth. Bring to a boil, then reduce the heat and simmer for 20 minutes.
Season with black pepper and stir in the parsley.
Puree the soup with an immersion blender until smooth.

Nutritional Information (per serving):
Calories: 120 kcal, Fat: 4g (0.14 oz), Carbs: 20g (0.7 oz), Protein: 2g (0.07 oz), Sodium: 50mg, Potassium: 300mg, Phosphorus: 50mg

Storage: Store leftovers in an airtight container in the refrigerator for up to 3 days.

Presentation: Serve in bowls with a sprinkle of fresh parsley.

Variations: Add a small amount of chopped garlic for extra flavor.

140. PEA AND MINT SOUP

Preparation Time: 10 minutes
Cooking Time: 15 minutes
Servings: 4

Ingredients:
- Frozen peas: 3 cups (450g / 1 lb)
- Fresh mint leaves, chopped: 2 tbsp (6g / 0.21 oz)
- Low-sodium vegetable broth: 4 cups (1 litre / 34 fl oz)
- Black pepper: 1/4 tsp (0.5g / 0.02 oz)
- Extra virgin olive oil: 1 tbsp (15ml / 0.5 oz)

Directions:
In a large pot, bring the vegetable broth to a boil. Add the peas and cook for 5 minutes.
Remove from heat and stir in the mint leaves and black pepper.
Puree the soup with an immersion blender until smooth.
Drizzle with olive oil before serving.

Nutritional Information (per serving):
Calories: 110 kcal, Fat: 4g (0.14 oz), Carbs: 16g (0.56 oz), Protein: 4g (0.14 oz), Sodium: 50mg, Potassium: 250mg, Phosphorus: 50mg

Storage: Store leftovers in an airtight container in the refrigerator for up to 3 days.

Presentation: Serve in bowls with a drizzle of olive oil and a sprig of fresh mint.

Variations: Add a squeeze of lemon juice before serving for extra brightness.

141. CARROT AND CORIANDER SOUP

Preparation Time: 15 minutes
Cooking Time: 25 minutes
Servings: 4

Ingredients:
- Carrots, peeled and chopped: 4 (400g / 14 oz)
- Onion, chopped: 1 (100g / 3.5 oz)
- Fresh coriander, chopped: 2 tbsp (6g / 0.21 oz)
- Low-sodium vegetable broth: 4 cups (1 litre / 34 fl oz)
- Black pepper: 1/4 tsp (0.5g / 0.02 oz)
- Extra virgin olive oil: 1 tbsp (15ml / 0.5 oz)

Directions:
Heat the olive oil in a large pot over medium heat.
Add the onion and cook until softened, about 5 minutes.
Add the carrots and vegetable broth, and bring to a boil.
Reduce heat and simmer for 20 minutes, until the carrots are tender.
Stir in the coriander and black pepper, then puree with an immersion blender until smooth.

Nutritional Information (per serving):
Calories: 100 kcal, Fat: 4g (0.14 oz), Carbs: 16g (0.56 oz), Protein: 2g (0.07 oz), Sodium: 50mg, Potassium: 300mg, Phosphorus: 40mg

Storage: Store leftovers in an airtight container in the refrigerator for up to 3 days.

Presentation: Serve in bowls garnished with fresh coriander.

Variations: Add a small amount of grated ginger for extra flavor.

142. CREAMY CAULIFLOWER SOUP

Preparation Time: 15 minutes
Cooking Time: 25 minutes
Servings: 4

Ingredients:
- Cauliflower, chopped: 1 medium head (600g / 21 oz)
- Onion, chopped: 1 (100g / 3.5 oz)
- Low-sodium vegetable broth: 4 cups (1 litre / 34 fl oz)
- Black pepper: 1/4 tsp (0.5g / 0.02 oz)
- Extra virgin olive oil: 1 tbsp (15ml / 0.5 oz)

Directions:
Heat the olive oil in a large pot over medium heat.
Add the onion and cook until softened, about 5 minutes.
Add the cauliflower and vegetable broth, and bring to a boil.
Reduce heat and simmer for 20 minutes, until the cauliflower is tender.
Puree the soup with an immersion blender until smooth.
Season with black pepper to taste.

Nutritional Information (per serving):
Calories: 90 kcal, Fat: 4g (0.14 oz), Carbs: 12g (0.42 oz), Protein: 3g (0.11 oz), Sodium: 50mg, Potassium: 300mg, Phosphorus: 40mg

Storage: Store leftovers in an airtight container in the refrigerator for up to 3 days.

Presentation: Serve in bowls garnished with a drizzle of olive oil.

Variations: Add a small amount of nutmeg for extra flavor.

143. ROASTED TOMATO SOUP

Preparation Time: 10 minutes
Cooking Time: 30 minutes
Servings: 4

Ingredients:
- Tomatoes, halved: 8 (800g / 28 oz)
- Onion, chopped: 1 (100g / 3.5 oz)
- Garlic, minced: 2 cloves (6g / 0.21 oz)
- Low-sodium vegetable broth: 4 cups (1 litre / 34 fl oz)
- Black pepper: 1/4 tsp (0.5g / 0.02 oz)
- Extra virgin olive oil: 2 tbsp (30ml / 1 oz)

Directions:
Preheat the oven to 400°F (200°C / Gas Mark 6). Place the tomatoes and onions on a baking sheet and drizzle with olive oil.
Roast for 25 minutes, until the tomatoes are soft.
In a large pot, heat the garlic for 1 minute.
Add the roasted tomatoes and onions, vegetable broth, and black pepper.
Bring to a boil, then reduce heat and simmer for 5 minutes.
Puree the soup with an immersion blender until smooth.

Nutritional Information (per serving):
Calories: 110 kcal, Fat: 6g (0.21 oz), Carbs: 14g (0.49 oz), Protein: 3g (0.11 oz), Sodium: 50mg, Potassium: 400mg, Phosphorus: 50mg

Storage: Store leftovers in an airtight container in the refrigerator for up to 3 days.

Presentation: Serve in bowls with a drizzle of olive oil and fresh basil leaves.

Variations: Add a pinch of red pepper flakes for a spicy kick.

FRIED STARTERS

144. BLACK PUDDING BONBONS

Preparation Time: 20 minutes
Cooking Time: 10 minutes
Servings: 6

Ingredients:
- Black pudding, crumbled: 1 cup (200g / 7 oz)
- Mashed potato: 1 cup (150g / 5.3 oz)
- Low-sodium breadcrumbs: 1/2 cup (60g / 2.1 oz)
- Egg, beaten: 1
- Black pepper: 1/4 tsp (0.5g / 0.02 oz)
- Extra virgin olive oil: 2 tbsp (30ml / 1 oz)

Directions:
In a bowl, mix the crumbled black pudding, mashed potato, and black pepper.
Form the mixture into small balls.

Roll the balls in flour, then dip in the beaten egg, and coat with breadcrumbs.

Heat the olive oil in a frying pan and cook the bonbons until golden brown, about 5 minutes per side.

Nutritional Information (per serving):
Calories: 190 kcal, Fat: 12g (0.42 oz), Carbs: 14g (0.49 oz), Protein: 6g (0.21 oz), Sodium: 180mg, Potassium: 200mg, Phosphorus: 70mg

Storage: Store leftovers in an airtight container in the refrigerator for up to 2 days.

Presentation: Serve on a platter with a garnish of fresh parsley.

Variations: Use a mixture of different herbs and spices for a varied flavor.

145. SPICED PARSNIP FRITTERS

Preparation Time: 15 minutes
Cooking Time: 15 minutes
Servings: 6

Ingredients:
- Parsnips, grated: 2 cups (300g / 10.5 oz)
- All-purpose flour: 1/2 cup (60g / 2.1 oz)
- Egg, beaten: 1
- Ground cumin: 1/2 tsp (1g / 0.04 oz)
- Ground coriander: 1/2 tsp (1g / 0.04 oz)
- Black pepper: 1/4 tsp (0.5g / 0.02 oz)
- Extra virgin olive oil: 2 tbsp (30ml / 1 oz)

Directions:
In a bowl, combine the grated parsnips, flour, egg, cumin, coriander, and black pepper.

Heat the olive oil in a frying pan over medium heat.

Drop spoonfuls of the mixture into the pan, flattening slightly.

Cook for 3-4 minutes per side, until golden brown.

Nutritional Information (per serving):
Calories: 90 kcal, Fat: 4g (0.14 oz), Carbs: 12g (0.42 oz), Protein: 2g (0.07 oz), Sodium: 20mg, Potassium: 250mg, Phosphorus: 40mg

Storage: Store leftovers in an airtight container in the refrigerator for up to 2 days.

Presentation: Serve on a platter with a garnish of fresh herbs.

Variations: Add a small amount of chopped onion for extra flavor.

146. FRIED VEGETABLE BALLS

Preparation Time: 20 minutes
Cooking Time: 15 minutes
Servings: 4

Ingredients:
- Carrots, grated: 2 (200g / 7 oz)
- Courgettes, grated: 2 (200g / 7 oz)
- Onion, finely chopped: 1 (100g / 3.5 oz)
- Garlic, minced: 1 clove (3g / 0.11 oz)
- Chickpea flour: 1 cup (120g / 4.2 oz)
- Ground cumin: 1 tsp (2g / 0.07 oz)
- Black pepper: 1/4 tsp (0.5g / 0.02 oz)
- Extra virgin olive oil: for frying

Directions:
In a large bowl, mix the grated carrots, courgettes, onion, garlic, chickpea flour, cumin, and black pepper.

Form the mixture into small balls.

Heat the olive oil in a frying pan over medium heat.

Fry the vegetable balls in batches until golden brown, about 5 minutes per batch.

Drain on paper towels before serving.

Nutritional Information (per serving):
Calories: 160 kcal, Fat: 8g (0.28 oz), Carbs: 18g (0.63 oz), Protein: 5g (0.18 oz), Sodium: 30mg, Potassium: 250mg, Phosphorus: 70mg

Storage: Best enjoyed fresh. Store leftovers in an airtight container in the refrigerator for up to 1 day.

Presentation: Serve on a platter with a yogurt dip.

Variations: Add grated beetroot for a different flavor and color.

147. FRIED SWEET POTATO WEDGES

Preparation Time: 10 minutes
Cooking Time: 20 minutes
Servings: 4

Ingredients:
- Sweet potatoes, cut into wedges: 2 large (600g / 21 oz)
- Extra virgin olive oil: 3 tbsp (45ml / 1.5 oz)
- Paprika: 1 tsp (2g / 0.07 oz)
- Black pepper: 1/4 tsp (0.5g / 0.02 oz)

Directions:
Preheat the oven to 200°C (400°F / Gas Mark 6).
In a large bowl, toss the sweet potato wedges with olive oil, paprika, and black pepper.
Arrange the wedges on a baking sheet in a single layer.
Bake for 20 minutes, turning halfway through, until golden and crispy.

Nutritional Information (per serving):
Calories: 180 kcal, Fat: 7g (0.25 oz), Carbs: 28g (0.98 oz), Protein: 2g (0.07 oz), Sodium: 30mg, Potassium: 450mg, Phosphorus: 40mg

Storage: Best enjoyed fresh. Store leftovers in an airtight container in the refrigerator for up to 1 day.

Presentation: Serve on a platter with a sprinkle of paprika.

Variations: Add a dash of cinnamon for a sweet twist.

148. MINI SCOTCH EGGS

Preparation Time: 20 minutes
Cooking Time: 20 minutes
Servings: 6

Ingredients:
- Quail eggs: 12
- Lean minced pork: 1 lb (450g)
- Fresh parsley, chopped: 2 tbsp (6g / 0.21 oz)
- Fresh thyme, chopped: 1 tbsp (1.5g / 0.05 oz)
- Black pepper: 1/4 tsp (0.5g / 0.02 oz)
- Low-sodium breadcrumbs: 1/2 cup (60g / 2.1 oz)
- All-purpose flour: 1/2 cup (60g / 2.1 oz)
- Egg, beaten: 1
- Extra virgin olive oil: 1 tbsp (15ml / 0.5 oz)

Directions:
Preheat the oven to 400°F (200°C).
Boil the quail eggs for 4 minutes, then cool under cold water and peel.
In a bowl, mix the minced pork, parsley, thyme, and black pepper.
Divide the mixture into 12 portions and flatten each one.
Wrap each portion around a quail egg, shaping into a ball.
Roll the balls in flour, then dip in the beaten egg, and coat with breadcrumbs.
Place on a baking sheet and drizzle with olive oil.
Bake for 20 minutes or until golden brown.

Nutritional Information (per serving):
Calories: 180 kcal, Fat: 10g (0.35 oz), Carbs: 8g (0.28 oz), Protein: 14g (0.5 oz), Sodium: 150mg, Potassium: 250mg, Phosphorus: 140mg

Storage: Store leftovers in an airtight container in the refrigerator for up to 3 days.

Presentation: Serve on a platter garnished with fresh parsley.

Variations: Use ground turkey or chicken instead of pork for a different flavor.

149. BUBBLE AND SQUEAK CAKES

Preparation Time: 15 minutes
Cooking Time: 20 minutes
Servings: 6

Ingredients:
- Potatoes, peeled and cubed: 2 cups (300g / 10.5 oz)
- Shredded cabbage: 1 cup (100g / 3.5 oz)
- Carrots, grated: 1/2 cup (50g / 1.75 oz)
- Extra virgin olive oil: 2 tbsp (30ml / 1 oz)
- Fresh parsley, chopped: 2 tbsp (6g / 0.21 oz)
- Black pepper: 1/4 tsp (0.5g / 0.02 oz)

Directions:
Boil the potatoes until tender, then mash them.
Sauté the cabbage and carrots in 1 tbsp of olive oil until softened.
Combine the mashed potatoes, sautéed vegetables, parsley, and black pepper.
Form the mixture into patties.
Heat the remaining olive oil in a frying pan and cook the patties until golden brown on both sides, about 5 minutes per side.

Nutritional Information (per serving):
Calories: 100 kcal, Fat: 5g (0.18 oz), Carbs: 12g (0.42 oz), Protein: 2g (0.07 oz), Sodium: 30mg, Potassium: 250mg, Phosphorus: 40mg

Storage: Store leftovers in an airtight container in the refrigerator for up to 2 days.

Presentation: Serve with a side of fresh parsley.

Variations: Add a small amount of finely chopped onion for extra flavor.

BAKED STARTERS

150. MINI TOAD IN THE HOLE

Preparation Time: 15 minutes
Cooking Time: 25 minutes
Servings: 6

Ingredients:
- Mini sausages: 12 (300g / 10.5 oz)
- All-purpose flour: 1 cup (120g / 4.2 oz)
- Milk: 1 cup (240ml / 8 oz)
- Egg: 1
- Black pepper: 1/4 tsp (0.5g / 0.02 oz)
- Extra virgin olive oil: 2 tbsp (30ml / 1 oz)

Directions:
Preheat the oven to 425°F (220°C).
Cook the mini sausages in a frying pan until browned, then set aside.
In a bowl, mix the flour, milk, egg, and black pepper to form a batter.
Add 1 tbsp of olive oil to a muffin tin and heat in the oven for 5 minutes.
Divide the sausages among the muffin cups, then pour the batter over them.

Bake for 20-25 minutes or until the batter is puffed and golden.

Nutritional Information (per serving):
Calories: 160 kcal, Fat: 9g (0.32 oz), Carbs: 12g (0.42 oz), Protein: 6g (0.21 oz), Sodium: 180mg, Potassium: 140mg, Phosphorus: 90mg

Storage: Store leftovers in an airtight container in the refrigerator for up to 2 days.

Presentation: Serve with a side of low-sodium gravy for dipping.

Variations: Use vegetarian sausages for a meat-free version.

151. WELSH RAREBIT BITES

Preparation Time: 10 minutes
Cooking Time: 10 minutes
Servings: 6

Ingredients:
- Wholemeal bread slices, cut into quarters: 6 (150g / 5.3 oz)
- Low-fat cheddar cheese, grated: 1 cup (120g / 4.2 oz)
- Low-sodium mustard: 1 tsp (5g / 0.18 oz)
- Worcestershire sauce (low-sodium): 1 tsp (5ml / 0.18 oz)
- Black pepper: 1/4 tsp (0.5g / 0.02 oz)

Directions:
Preheat the oven to 400°F (200°C).
In a bowl, mix the grated cheese, mustard, Worcestershire sauce, and black pepper.
Spread the cheese mixture over the bread quarters.
Place on a baking sheet and bake for 10 minutes, or until the cheese is melted and bubbly.

Nutritional Information (per serving):
Calories: 140 kcal, Fat: 8g (0.28 oz), Carbs: 12g (0.42 oz), Protein: 6g (0.21 oz), Sodium: 180mg, Potassium: 100mg, Phosphorus: 100mg

Storage: Best enjoyed fresh. Store leftovers in an airtight container in the refrigerator for up to 1 day.

Presentation: Serve on a platter with a sprinkle of black pepper.

Variations: Use a mixture of different cheeses for a varied flavor.

152. CORNISH PASTY BITES

Preparation Time: 25 minutes
Cooking Time: 25 minutes
Servings: 6

Ingredients:
- Lean beef mince: 1/2 lb (225g)
- Potato, finely diced: 1/2 cup (75g / 2.6 oz)
- Swede (rutabaga), finely diced: 1/2 cup (75g / 2.6 oz)
- Carrot, finely diced: 1/2 cup (75g / 2.6 oz)
- Black pepper: 1/4 tsp (0.5g / 0.02 oz)
- Wholemealshortcrust pastry: 1 sheet (200g / 7 oz)
- Extra virgin olive oil: 1 tbsp (15ml / 0.5 oz)

Directions:
Preheat the oven to 400°F (200°C).
In a frying pan, cook the beef mince until browned, then add the diced potato, swede, carrot, and black pepper. Cook until the vegetables are tender.
Roll out the pastry and cut into small circles.
Place a spoonful of the meat mixture onto each pastry circle and fold to seal.

Brush with olive oil and bake for 20-25 minutes, until golden brown.

Nutritional Information (per serving):
Calories: 200 kcal, Fat: 10g (0.35 oz), Carbs: 18g (0.63 oz), Protein: 8g (0.28 oz), Sodium: 150mg, Potassium: 200mg, Phosphorus: 80mg

Storage: Store leftovers in an airtight container in the refrigerator for up to 2 days.

Presentation: Serve on a platter garnished with fresh herbs.

Variations: Use ground turkey or chicken instead of beef for a different flavor.

153. MINI SHEPHERD'S PIES

Preparation Time: 20 minutes
Cooking Time: 30 minutes
Servings: 6

Ingredients:
- Lean lamb mince: 1/2 lb (225g)
- Onion, finely chopped: 1/2 (50g / 1.75 oz)
- Carrot, finely chopped: 1/2 cup (50g / 1.75 oz)
- Peas: 1/2 cup (75g / 2.6 oz)
- Black pepper: 1/4 tsp (0.5g / 0.02 oz)
- Potato, mashed: 2 cups (300g / 10.5 oz)
- Extra virgin olive oil: 1 tbsp (15ml / 0.5 oz)

Directions:
Preheat the oven to 400°F (200°C).
In a frying pan, cook the lamb mince with the onion and carrot until browned.
Add the peas and black pepper, then cook for another 5 minutes.
Divide the mixture among small ramekins and top with mashed potato.

Brush with olive oil and bake for 20-25 minutes, until the tops are golden brown.

Nutritional Information (per serving):
Calories: 250 kcal, Fat: 12g (0.42 oz), Carbs: 18g (0.63 oz), Protein: 14g (0.5 oz), Sodium: 150mg, Potassium: 350mg, Phosphorus: 140mg

Storage: Store leftovers in an airtight container in the refrigerator for up to 2 days.

Presentation: Serve in the ramekins with a garnish of fresh parsley.

Variations: Use ground beef or turkey instead of lamb for a different flavor.

154. MUSHROOM AND SPINACH TARTLETS

Preparation Time: 20 minutes
Cooking Time: 25 minutes
Servings: 6

Ingredients:
- Wholemeal pastry: 1 sheet (200g / 7 oz)
- Mushrooms, sliced: 1 cup (100g / 3.5 oz)
- Fresh spinach, chopped: 1 cup (30g / 1 oz)
- Low-fat cream cheese: 1/2 cup (120g / 4.2 oz)
- Black pepper: 1/4 tsp (0.5g / 0.02 oz)
- Extra virgin olive oil: 1 tbsp (15ml / 0.5 oz)

Directions:
Preheat the oven to 375°F (190°C).
Roll out the pastry and cut into small circles. Place the circles into a greased muffin tin.
In a frying pan, heat the olive oil and cook the mushrooms until softened. Add the spinach and cook until wilted.
Mix the cooked mushrooms and spinach with the cream cheese and black pepper.

Spoon the mixture into the pastry circles.
Bake for 20-25 minutes, until the pastry is golden brown.

Nutritional Information (per serving):
Calories: 170 kcal, Fat: 10g (0.35 oz), Carbs: 16g (0.56 oz), Protein: 4g (0.14 oz), Sodium: 140mg, Potassium: 150mg, Phosphorus: 60mg

Storage: Store leftovers in an airtight container in the refrigerator for up to 2 days.

Presentation: Serve on a platter with a garnish of fresh herbs.

Variations: Use feta cheese instead of cream cheese for a different flavor.

COLD STARTERS

SEAFOOD STARTERS

155. SMOKED SALMON AND DILL BITES

Preparation Time: 10 minutes
Servings: 4

Ingredients:
- Smoked salmon slices: 200g (7 oz)
- Low-fat cream cheese: 1/2 cup (120g / 4.2 oz)
- Fresh dill, chopped: 2 tbsp (6g / 0.21 oz)
- Lemon zest: 1 tsp (2g / 0.07 oz)
- Black pepper: 1/4 tsp (0.5g / 0.02 oz)
- Wholemeal crackers: 16

Directions:

In a bowl, mix the cream cheese, dill, lemon zest, and black pepper.
Spread the mixture on the crackers.
Top each cracker with a slice of smoked salmon.

Nutritional Information (per serving):
Calories: 140 kcal, Fat: 8g (0.28 oz), Carbs: 10g (0.35 oz), Protein: 8g (0.28 oz), Sodium: 180mg, Potassium: 150mg, Phosphorus: 90mg

Storage: Best enjoyed fresh. Store leftovers in an airtight container in the refrigerator for up to 1 day.

Presentation: Serve on a platter garnished with fresh dill.

Variations: Use goat cheese instead of cream cheese for a different flavor.

156. SHRIMP COCKTAIL

Preparation Time: 15 minutes
Servings: 4

Ingredients:
- Cooked shrimp, peeled and deveined: 200g (7 oz)
- Low-sodium cocktail sauce: 1/2 cup (120ml / 4.2 oz)
- Lemon wedges: 4
- Fresh parsley, chopped: 2 tbsp (6g / 0.21 oz)

Directions:
Arrange the shrimp on a serving platter.
Serve with cocktail sauce and lemon wedges.
Garnish with chopped parsley.

Nutritional Information (per serving):
Calories: 90 kcal, Fat: 1g (0.04 oz), Carbs: 8g (0.28 oz), Protein: 14g (0.49 oz), Sodium: 150mg, Potassium: 200mg, Phosphorus: 100mg

Storage: Best enjoyed fresh. Store leftovers in an airtight container in the refrigerator for up to 1 day.

Presentation: Serve on a platter with lemon wedges and a bowl of cocktail sauce.

Variations: Add a dash of hot sauce to the cocktail sauce for a spicy kick.

157. CRAB AND AVOCADO TARTARE

Preparation Time: 15 minutes
Servings: 4

Ingredients:
- Cooked crab meat: 200g (7 oz)
- Avocado, diced: 1 (150g / 5.3 oz)
- Lime juice: 2 tbsp (30ml / 1 oz)
- Fresh coriander, chopped: 2 tbsp (6g / 0.21 oz)
- Black pepper: 1/4 tsp (0.5g / 0.02 oz)

Directions:
In a bowl, gently mix the crab meat, diced avocado, lime juice, coriander, and black pepper.
Divide the mixture among small serving dishes.

Nutritional Information (per serving):
Calories: 130 kcal, Fat: 7g (0.25 oz), Carbs: 5g (0.18 oz), Protein: 13g (0.46 oz), Sodium: 160mg, Potassium: 300mg, Phosphorus: 100mg

Storage: Best enjoyed fresh. Store leftovers in an airtight container in the refrigerator for up to 1 day.

Presentation: Serve in small dishes garnished with fresh coriander.

Variations: Add a few diced cherry tomatoes for extra color and flavor.

158. TUNA AND CUCUMBER CUPS

Preparation Time: 10 minutes
Servings: 4

Ingredients:
- Cucumber, cut into 1-inch slices: 1 large (300g / 10.5 oz)
- Canned tuna in water, drained: 1 can (120g / 4.2 oz)
- Low-fat Greek yogurt: 2 tbsp (30ml / 1 oz)
- Fresh dill, chopped: 1 tbsp (3g / 0.1 oz)
- Lemon juice: 1 tbsp (15ml / 0.5 oz)
- Black pepper: 1/4 tsp (0.5g / 0.02 oz)

Directions:
Scoop out a small portion of the center of each cucumber slice to create a cup.
In a bowl, mix the tuna, Greek yogurt, dill, lemon juice, and black pepper.
Spoon the tuna mixture into the cucumber cups.

Nutritional Information (per serving):
Calories: 70 kcal, Fat: 2g (0.07 oz), Carbs: 5g (0.18 oz), Protein: 10g (0.35 oz), Sodium: 100mg, Potassium: 150mg, Phosphorus: 90mg

Storage: Best enjoyed fresh. Store leftovers in an airtight container in the refrigerator for up to 1 day.

Presentation: Arrange the cucumber cups on a platter and garnish with fresh dill.

Variations: Use crab meat or smoked salmon instead of tuna for a different flavor.

159. SMOKED MACKEREL PÂTÉ

Preparation Time: 10 minutes

Servings: 4

Ingredients:
- Smoked mackerel fillets, skin removed: 200g (7 oz)
- Low-fat cream cheese: 1/2 cup (120g / 4.2 oz)
- Lemon juice: 2 tbsp (30ml / 1 oz)
- Fresh chives, chopped: 2 tbsp (6g / 0.21 oz)
- Black pepper: 1/4 tsp (0.5g / 0.02 oz)
- Wholemeal bread slices, toasted: 4

Directions:
In a bowl, blend the mackerel fillets, cream cheese, lemon juice, chives, and black pepper until smooth. Serve with toasted wholemeal bread.

Nutritional Information (per serving):
Calories: 150 kcal, Fat: 9g (0.32 oz), Carbs: 8g (0.28 oz), Protein: 10g (0.35 oz), Sodium: 200mg, Potassium: 180mg, Phosphorus: 100mg

Storage: Store leftovers in an airtight container in the refrigerator for up to 2 days.

Presentation: Serve on a platter with toasted bread and a sprinkle of fresh chives.

Variations: Use smoked trout or salmon instead of mackerel for a different flavor.

SALAD STARTERS

160. ROCKET AND PEAR SALAD

Preparation Time: 10 minutes
Servings: 4

Ingredients:
- Fresh rocket (arugula): 4 cups (120g / 4.2 oz)
- Pears, thinly sliced: 2 (300g / 10.5 oz)
- Walnuts, chopped: 1/4 cup (30g / 1 oz)
- Extra virgin olive oil: 2 tbsp (30ml / 1 oz)
- Lemon juice: 1 tbsp (15ml / 0.5 oz)
- Black pepper: 1/4 tsp (0.5g / 0.02 oz)

Directions:
In a large bowl, combine the rocket, pear slices, and walnuts.
In a small bowl, whisk together the olive oil, lemon juice, and black pepper.
Drizzle the dressing over the salad and toss to combine.

Nutritional Information (per serving):
Calories: 130 kcal, Fat: 9g (0.32 oz), Carbs: 11g (0.39 oz), Protein: 2g (0.07 oz), Sodium: 10mg, Potassium: 200mg, Phosphorus: 30mg

Storage: Best enjoyed fresh. Store leftovers in an airtight container in the refrigerator for up to 1 day.

Presentation: Serve in individual bowls with a sprinkle of chopped walnuts.

Variations: Add a small amount of crumbled blue cheese for extra flavor.

161. CUCUMBER AND RADISH SALAD

Preparation Time: 10 minutes
Servings: 4

Ingredients:
- Cucumber, thinly sliced: 1 large (300g / 10.5 oz)
- Radishes, thinly sliced: 1 cup (100g / 3.5 oz)
- Fresh dill, chopped: 2 tbsp (6g / 0.21 oz)
- Greek yogurt: 1/2 cup (120g / 4.2 oz)

- Lemon juice: 1 tbsp (15ml / 0.5 oz)
- Black pepper: 1/4 tsp (0.5g / 0.02 oz)

Directions:
In a large bowl, combine the cucumber, radishes, and dill.
In a small bowl, whisk together the Greek yogurt, lemon juice, and black pepper.
Pour the dressing over the vegetables and toss to combine.

Nutritional Information (per serving):
Calories: 50 kcal, Fat: 2g (0.07 oz), Carbs: 6g (0.21 oz), Protein: 2g (0.07 oz), Sodium: 20mg, Potassium: 150mg, Phosphorus: 30mg

Storage: Best enjoyed fresh. Store leftovers in an airtight container in the refrigerator for up to 1 day.

Presentation: Serve in individual bowls with a sprinkle of fresh dill.

Variations: Add thinly sliced red onion for extra flavor.

162. TOMATO AND BASIL SALAD

Preparation Time: 10 minutes
Servings: 4

Ingredients:
- Cherry tomatoes, halved: 2 cups (300g / 10.5 oz)
- Fresh basil leaves, torn: 1/4 cup (10g / 0.35 oz)
- Extra virgin olive oil: 2 tbsp (30ml / 1 oz)
- Balsamic vinegar: 1 tbsp (15ml / 0.5 oz)
- Black pepper: 1/4 tsp (0.5g / 0.02 oz)

Directions:
In a large bowl, combine the cherry tomatoes and basil leaves.
In a small bowl, whisk together the olive oil, balsamic vinegar, and black pepper.
Drizzle the dressing over the salad and toss to combine.

Nutritional Information (per serving):
Calories: 80 kcal, Fat: 6g (0.21 oz), Carbs: 6g (0.21 oz), Protein: 1g (0.04 oz), Sodium: 10mg, Potassium: 200mg, Phosphorus: 20mg

Storage: Best enjoyed fresh. Store leftovers in an airtight container in the refrigerator for up to 1 day.

Presentation: Serve in individual bowls with a drizzle of balsamic vinegar.

Variations: Add slices of fresh mozzarella for a Caprese-style salad.

163. BEETROOT AND FETA SALAD

Preparation Time: 10 minutes
Servings: 4

Ingredients:
- Cooked beetroot, diced: 2 cups (300g / 10.5 oz)
- Low-fat feta cheese, crumbled: 1/2 cup (60g / 2.1 oz)
- Fresh parsley, chopped: 2 tbsp (6g / 0.21 oz)
- Extra virgin olive oil: 2 tbsp (30ml / 1 oz)
- Lemon juice: 1 tbsp (15ml / 0.5 oz)
- Black pepper: 1/4 tsp (0.5g / 0.02 oz)

Directions:
In a large bowl, combine the beetroot, feta cheese, and parsley.

In a small bowl, whisk together the olive oil, lemon juice, and black pepper.
Drizzle the dressing over the salad and toss to combine.

Nutritional Information (per serving):
Calories: 120 kcal, Fat: 8g (0.28 oz), Carbs: 8g (0.28 oz), Protein: 4g (0.14 oz), Sodium: 150mg, Potassium: 200mg, Phosphorus: 40mg

Storage: Best enjoyed fresh. Store leftovers in an airtight container in the refrigerator for up to 1 day.

Presentation: Serve in individual bowls with a sprinkle of fresh parsley.

Variations: Add a small amount of chopped walnuts for extra texture.

164. MIXED BERRY AND SPINACH SALAD

Preparation Time: 10 minutes
Servings: 4

Ingredients:
- Freshspinach: 4 cups (120g / 4.2 oz)
- Mixed berries (strawberries, blueberries, raspberries): 2 cups (300g / 10.5 oz)
- Walnuts, chopped: 1/4 cup (30g / 1 oz)
- Extra virgin olive oil: 2 tbsp (30ml / 1 oz)
- Balsamic vinegar: 1 tbsp (15ml / 0.5 oz)
- Black pepper: 1/4 tsp (0.5g / 0.02 oz)

Directions:
In a large bowl, combine the spinach, mixed berries, and walnuts.
In a small bowl, whisk together the olive oil, balsamic vinegar, and black pepper.
Drizzle the dressing over the salad and toss to combine.

Nutritional Information (per serving):
Calories: 120 kcal, Fat: 8g (0.28 oz), Carbs: 10g (0.35 oz), Protein: 2g (0.07 oz), Sodium: 10mg, Potassium: 200mg, Phosphorus: 30mg

Storage: Best enjoyed fresh. Store leftovers in an airtight container in the refrigerator for up to 1 day.

Presentation: Serve in individual bowls with a sprinkle of chopped walnuts.

Variations: Add a small amount of crumbled feta cheese for extra flavor.

VEGETABLE STARTERS

165. STUFFED CHERRY TOMATOES

Preparation Time: 15 minutes
Servings: 4

Ingredients:
- Cherry tomatoes, halved and seeds removed: 2 cups (300g / 10.5 oz)
- Low-fat ricotta cheese: 1/2 cup (120g / 4.2 oz)
- Fresh basil, chopped: 2 tbsp (6g / 0.21 oz)
- Black pepper: 1/4 tsp (0.5g / 0.02 oz)

Directions:
In a bowl, mix the ricotta cheese, basil, and black pepper.
Stuff each cherry tomato half with the ricotta mixture.
Arrange on a serving platter.

Nutritional Information (per serving):
Calories: 70 kcal, Fat: 3g (0.11 oz), Carbs: 7g (0.25 oz), Protein: 3g (0.11 oz), Sodium: 40mg, Potassium: 250mg, Phosphorus: 40mg

Storage: Best enjoyed fresh. Store leftovers in an airtight container in the refrigerator for up to 1 day.

Presentation: Serve on a platter garnished with fresh basil leaves.

Variations: Use low-fat cottage cheese instead of ricotta for a different texture.

166. CUCUMBER AND AVOCADO ROLLS

Preparation Time: 10 minutes
Servings: 4

Ingredients:
- Cucumber, thinly sliced lengthwise: 1 large (300g / 10.5 oz)
- Avocado, mashed: 1 (150g / 5.3 oz)
- Fresh coriander, chopped: 2 tbsp (6g / 0.21 oz)
- Lime juice: 1 tbsp (15ml / 0.5 oz)
- Black pepper: 1/4 tsp (0.5g / 0.02 oz)

Directions:
In a bowl, mix the mashed avocado, coriander, lime juice, and black pepper.
Spread the avocado mixture onto each cucumber slice and roll up.
Secure with a toothpick if needed.

Nutritional Information (per serving):
Calories: 60 kcal, Fat: 4g (0.14 oz), Carbs: 6g (0.21 oz), Protein: 1g (0.04 oz), Sodium: 5mg, Potassium: 250mg, Phosphorus: 30mg

Storage: Best enjoyed fresh. Store leftovers in an airtight container in the refrigerator for up to 1 day.

Presentation: Serve on a platter with a sprinkle of fresh coriander.

Variations: Add a slice of smoked salmon to each roll for extra flavor.

167. BELL PEPPER AND HUMMUS CUPS

Preparation Time: 10 minutes
Servings: 4

Ingredients:
- Bell peppers, cut into bite-sized pieces: 2 (300g / 10.5 oz)
- Low-sodium hummus: 1/2 cup (120g / 4.2 oz)
- Paprika: 1/4 tsp (0.5g / 0.02 oz)
- Fresh parsley, chopped: 2 tbsp (6g / 0.21 oz)

Directions:
Spoon a small amount of hummus onto each bell pepper piece.
Sprinkle with paprika and fresh parsley.

Nutritional Information (per serving):
Calories: 80 kcal, Fat: 4g (0.14 oz), Carbs: 10g (0.35 oz), Protein: 2g (0.07 oz), Sodium: 60mg, Potassium: 250mg, Phosphorus: 50mg

Storage: Best enjoyed fresh. Store leftovers in an airtight container in the refrigerator for up to 1 day.

Presentation: Serve on a platter garnished with fresh parsley.

Variations: Use different colored bell peppers for a vibrant presentation.

168. GRILLED VEGETABLE ANTIPASTO

Preparation Time: 15 minutes

Cooking Time: 10 minutes
Servings: 4

Ingredients:
- Aubergine, thinly sliced: 1 (300g / 10.5 oz)
- Courgette, thinly sliced: 1 (200g / 7 oz)
- Bell pepper, sliced: 1 (150g / 5.3 oz)
- Extra virgin olive oil: 2 tbsp (30ml / 1 oz)
- Fresh rosemary, chopped: 1 tbsp (1.5g / 0.05 oz)
- Black pepper: 1/4 tsp (0.5g / 0.02 oz)

Directions:
Preheat the grill to medium-high heat.
Brush the vegetables with olive oil and sprinkle with rosemary and black pepper.
Grill the vegetables for 3-4 minutes on each side, until tender and slightly charred.
Allow to cool before serving.

Nutritional Information (per serving):
Calories: 90 kcal, Fat: 5g (0.18 oz), Carbs: 10g (0.35 oz), Protein: 2g (0.07 oz), Sodium: 10mg, Potassium: 250mg, Phosphorus: 30mg

Storage: Store leftovers in an airtight container in the refrigerator for up to 2 days.

Presentation: Serve on a platter with a sprinkle of fresh rosemary.

Variations: Add grilled mushrooms for extra flavor.

169. ZUCCHINI RIBBONS WITH LEMON

Preparation Time: 10 minutes
Servings: 4

Ingredients:
- Zucchini, thinly sliced into ribbons: 2 (300g / 10.5 oz)
- Lemon juice: 2 tbsp (30ml / 1 oz)
- Extra virgin olive oil: 1 tbsp (15ml / 0.5 oz)
- Fresh mint, chopped: 2 tbsp (6g / 0.21 oz)
- Black pepper: 1/4 tsp (0.5g / 0.02 oz)

Directions:
In a large bowl, combine the zucchini ribbons, lemon juice, olive oil, mint, and black pepper. Toss gently to coat the zucchini.

Nutritional Information (per serving):
Calories: 50 kcal, Fat: 3g (0.11 oz), Carbs: 5g (0.18 oz), Protein: 1g (0.04 oz), Sodium: 5mg, Potassium: 200mg, Phosphorus: 20mg

Storage: Best enjoyed fresh. Store leftovers in an airtight container in the refrigerator for up to 1 day.

Presentation: Serve in a bowl with a sprinkle of fresh mint.

Variations: Add a small amount of crumbled feta cheese for extra flavor.

MEAT AND CHEESE STARTERS

170. PROSCIUTTO AND MELON BITES

Preparation Time: 10 minutes
Servings: 4

Ingredients:
- Melon, cut into bite-sized pieces: 1 cup (150g / 5.3 oz)
- Prosciutto slices: 8 (100g / 3.5 oz)
- Fresh basil leaves: 16
- Black pepper: 1/4 tsp (0.5g / 0.02 oz)

Directions:

Wrap each melon piece with a slice of prosciutto and a basil leaf.
Secure with a toothpick and sprinkle with black pepper.

Nutritional Information (per serving):
Calories: 80 kcal, Fat: 4g (0.14 oz), Carbs: 8g (0.28 oz), Protein: 5g (0.18 oz), Sodium: 200mg, Potassium: 200mg, Phosphorus: 40mg

Storage: Best enjoyed fresh. Store leftovers in an airtight container in the refrigerator for up to 1 day.
Presentation: Serve on a platter garnished with fresh basil.
Variations: Use different types of melon for a varied flavor.

171. TURKEY AND CHEESE ROLL-UPS

Preparation Time: 10 minutes
Servings: 4

Ingredients:
- Sliced turkey breast: 8 slices (200g / 7 oz)
- Low-fat cheddar cheese, cut into sticks: 8 (80g / 2.8 oz)
- Fresh spinach leaves: 16
- Black pepper: 1/4 tsp (0.5g / 0.02 oz)

Directions:
Place a cheese stick and two spinach leaves on each turkey slice.
Roll up tightly and secure with a toothpick.
Sprinkle with black pepper.

Nutritional Information (per serving):
Calories: 90 kcal, Fat: 4g (0.14 oz), Carbs: 1g (0.04 oz), Protein: 12g (0.42 oz), Sodium: 200mg, Potassium: 150mg, Phosphorus: 100mg

Storage: Best enjoyed fresh. Store leftovers in an airtight container in the refrigerator for up to 1 day.
Presentation: Arrange the roll-ups on a platter.
Variations: Use different types of cheese or add a slice of avocado for extra flavor.

172. BEEF AND BLUE CHEESE CROSTINI

Preparation Time: 10 minutes
Cooking Time: 5 minutes
Servings: 4

Ingredients:
- Wholemeal baguette, sliced: 8 pieces (100g / 3.5 oz)
- Cooked roast beef, thinly sliced: 100g (3.5 oz)
- Blue cheese, crumbled: 1/4 cup (30g / 1 oz)
- Fresh arugula (rocket): 1 cup (30g / 1 oz)
- Black pepper: 1/4 tsp (0.5g / 0.02 oz)

Directions:
Preheat the grill to high.
Toast the baguette slices under the grill for 1-2 minutes, until golden.
Top each slice with roast beef, blue cheese, and arugula.
Sprinkle with black pepper.

Nutritional Information (per serving):
Calories: 110 kcal, Fat: 5g (0.18 oz), Carbs: 10g (0.35 oz), Protein: 7g (0.25 oz), Sodium: 180mg, Potassium: 100mg, Phosphorus: 90mg

Storage: Best enjoyed fresh. Store leftovers in an airtight container in the refrigerator for up to 1 day.

Presentation: Serve on a platter with a sprinkle of fresh arugula.

Variations: Use goat cheese instead of blue cheese for a milder flavor.

173. HAM AND CREAM CHEESE ROLL-UPS

Preparation Time: 10 minutes
Servings: 4

Ingredients:
- Sliced ham: 8 slices (200g / 7 oz)
- Low-fat cream cheese: 1/2 cup (120g / 4.2 oz)
- Fresh chives, chopped: 2 tbsp (6g / 0.21 oz)
- Black pepper: 1/4 tsp (0.5g / 0.02 oz)

Directions:
Spread a thin layer of cream cheese on each slice of ham.
Sprinkle with chopped chives and black pepper.
Roll up tightly and slice into bite-sized pieces.

Nutritional Information (per serving):
Calories: 90 kcal, Fat: 6g (0.21 oz), Carbs: 1g (0.04 oz), Protein: 8g (0.28 oz), Sodium: 300mg, Potassium: 150mg, Phosphorus: 90mg

Storage: Best enjoyed fresh. Store leftovers in an airtight container in the refrigerator for up to 1 day.

Presentation: Arrange the roll-ups on a platter with a sprinkle of fresh chives.

Variations: Use turkey or chicken slices instead of ham for a different flavor.

174. CHICKEN AND AVOCADO SALAD CUPS

Preparation Time: 15 minutes
Servings: 4

Ingredients:
- Cooked chicken breast, diced: 1 cup (150g / 5.3 oz)
- Avocado, diced: 1 (150g / 5.3 oz)
- Fresh coriander, chopped: 2 tbsp (6g / 0.21 oz)
- Lime juice: 2 tbsp (30ml / 1 oz)
- Black pepper: 1/4 tsp (0.5g / 0.02 oz)
- Lettuce leaves: 8

Directions:
In a bowl, mix the chicken, avocado, coriander, lime juice, and black pepper.
Spoon the mixture into lettuce leaves to create cups.

Nutritional Information (per serving):
Calories: 120 kcal, Fat: 8g (0.28 oz), Carbs: 4g (0.14 oz), Protein: 10g (0.35 oz), Sodium: 60mg, Potassium: 250mg, Phosphorus: 100mg

Storage: Best enjoyed fresh. Store leftovers in an airtight container in the refrigerator for up to 1 day.

Presentation: Serve the lettuce cups on a platter with a sprinkle of fresh coriander.

Variations: Add a small amount of diced red onion for extra flavor.

175. MINI CAPRESE SKEWERS

Preparation Time: 10 minutes
Servings: 4

Ingredients:
- Cherry tomatoes: 20 (300g / 10.5 oz)
- Fresh mozzarella balls: 20 (150g / 5.3 oz)
- Fresh basil leaves: 20
- Balsamic glaze: 2 tbsp (30ml / 1 oz)
- Black pepper: 1/4 tsp (0.5g / 0.02 oz)

Directions:

Thread a cherry tomato, mozzarella ball, and basil leaf onto each skewer.

Drizzle with balsamic glaze and sprinkle with black pepper.

Nutritional Information (per serving):

Calories: 110 kcal, Fat: 7g (0.25 oz), Carbs: 5g (0.18 oz), Protein: 6g (0.21 oz), Sodium: 100mg, Potassium: 150mg, Phosphorus: 90mg

Storage: Best enjoyed fresh. Store leftovers in an airtight container in the refrigerator for up to 1 day.

Presentation: Serve on a platter with a drizzle of balsamic glaze.

Variations: Add a slice of prosciutto to each skewer for extra flavor.

Chapter 6: Soup

176. SCOTTISH BARLEY SOUP

Preparation Time: 15 minutes
Cooking Time: 60 minutes
Servings: 4

Ingredients:
- Pearl barley: 1/2 cup (100g / 3.5 oz)
- Carrots, diced: 2 (200g / 7 oz)
- Celery, diced: 2 stalks (100g / 3.5 oz)
- Onion, diced: 1 (100g / 3.5 oz)
- Leek, sliced: 1 (100g / 3.5 oz)
- Low-sodium vegetable broth: 6 cups (1.5 litres / 50 fl oz)
- Fresh thyme: 2 sprigs
- Black pepper: 1/4 tsp (0.5g / 0.02 oz)
- Fresh parsley, chopped: 2 tbsp (6g / 0.21 oz)

Directions:
Rinse the barley under cold water.
In a large pot, combine all ingredients except parsley.
Bring to a boil, then reduce heat and simmer for 60 minutes, until barley is tender.
Remove thyme sprigs and season with black pepper.
Garnish with fresh parsley before serving.

Nutritional Information (per serving):
Calories: 180 kcal, Fat: 1g (0.04 oz), Carbs: 37g (1.3 oz), Protein: 5g (0.18 oz), Sodium: 50mg, Potassium: 350mg, Phosphorus: 90mg

Storage: Store leftovers in an airtight container in the refrigerator for up to 3 days.

Presentation: Serve in bowls garnished with a sprig of parsley.

Variations: Add diced turnip or parsnip for additional flavor.

177. ENGLISH PEA AND HAM SOUP

Preparation Time: 15 minutes
Cooking Time: 30 minutes
Servings: 4

Ingredients:
- Frozen peas: 4 cups (600g / 1.3 lb)
- Low-sodium ham, diced: 1 cup (150g / 5.3 oz)
- Onion, diced: 1 (100g / 3.5 oz)
- Low-sodium vegetable broth: 4 cups (1 litre / 34 fl oz)
- Fresh mint leaves, chopped: 2 tbsp (6g / 0.21 oz)
- Black pepper: 1/4 tsp (0.5g / 0.02 oz)

Directions:
In a large pot, sauté the onion until softened.
Add the peas, ham, and vegetable broth.
Bring to a boil, then reduce heat and simmer for 20 minutes.
Stir in the mint leaves and season with black pepper.
Puree with an immersion blender until smooth.

Nutritional Information (per serving):
Calories: 220 kcal, Fat: 5g (0.18 oz), Carbs: 30g (1.1 oz), Protein: 14g (0.49 oz), Sodium: 150mg, Potassium: 400mg, Phosphorus: 150mg

Storage: Store leftovers in an airtight container in the refrigerator for up to 3 days.

Presentation: Serve in bowls with a sprinkle of chopped mint.

Variations: Use smoked turkey instead of ham for a different flavor.

178. LENTIL AND VEGETABLE SOUP

Preparation Time: 15 minutes
Cooking Time: 45 minutes
Servings: 4

Ingredients:

- Red lentils: 1 cup (200g / 7 oz)
- Carrots, diced: 2 (200g / 7 oz)
- Celery, diced: 2 stalks (100g / 3.5 oz)
- Onion, diced: 1 (100g / 3.5 oz)
- Tomato, diced: 2 (200g / 7 oz)
- Low-sodium vegetable broth: 6 cups (1.5 litres / 50 fl oz)
- Ground cumin: 1 tsp (2g / 0.07 oz)
- Black pepper: 1/4 tsp (0.5g / 0.02 oz)
- Fresh parsley, chopped: 2 tbsp (6g / 0.21 oz)

Directions:
Rinse the lentils under cold water.
In a large pot, combine all ingredients except parsley.
Bring to a boil, then reduce heat and simmer for 45 minutes, until lentils and vegetables are tender.
Season with black pepper and garnish with fresh parsley before serving.

Nutritional Information (per serving):
Calories: 250 kcal, Fat: 2g (0.07 oz), Carbs: 45g (1.6 oz), Protein: 15g (0.53 oz), Sodium: 50mg, Potassium: 500mg, Phosphorus: 200mg

Storage: Store leftovers in an airtight container in the refrigerator for up to 3 days.

Presentation: Serve in bowls garnished with a sprinkle of parsley.

Variations: Add a pinch of chili flakes for a spicy kick.

179. BROCCOLI AND CHEDDAR SOUP

Preparation Time: 15 minutes
Cooking Time: 30 minutes
Servings: 4

Ingredients:

- Broccoli florets: 4 cups (400g / 14 oz)
- Low-fat cheddar cheese, grated: 1 cup (120g / 4.2 oz)
- Onion, diced: 1 (100g / 3.5 oz)
- Low-sodium vegetable broth: 4 cups (1 litre / 34 fl oz)
- Black pepper: 1/4 tsp (0.5g / 0.02 oz)
- Low-fat milk: 1 cup (240ml / 8 oz)

Directions:
In a large pot, sauté the onion until softened.
Add the broccoli and vegetable broth, bring to a boil, then simmer for 20 minutes.
Puree with an immersion blender until smooth.
Stir in the grated cheddar and milk, and season with black pepper.
Heat through until the cheese is melted.

Nutritional Information (per serving):
Calories: 200 kcal, Fat: 8g (0.28 oz), Carbs: 20g (0.7 oz), Protein: 12g (0.42 oz), Sodium: 180mg, Potassium: 400mg, Phosphorus: 150mg

Storage: Store leftovers in an airtight container in the refrigerator for up to 3 days.

Presentation: Serve in bowls with a sprinkle of grated cheddar.

Variations: Add a handful of spinach for extra greens.

180. CREAMY PARSNIP SOUP

Preparation Time: 15 minutes
Cooking Time: 30 minutes
Servings: 4

Ingredients:
- Parsnips, peeled and diced: 4 (400g / 14 oz)
- Potato, peeled and diced: 1 (150g / 5.3 oz)
- Onion, diced: 1 (100g / 3.5 oz)
- Low-sodium vegetable broth: 6 cups (1.5 litres / 50 fl oz)
- Fresh thyme: 2 sprigs
- Black pepper: 1/4 tsp (0.5g / 0.02 oz)
- Low-fat milk: 1 cup (240ml / 8 oz)

Directions:
In a large pot, sauté the onion until softened.
Add the parsnips, potato, thyme, and vegetable broth.
Bring to a boil, then reduce heat and simmer for 25 minutes.
Remove thyme sprigs and puree with an immersion blender until smooth.
Stir in the milk and season with black pepper.

Nutritional Information (per serving):
Calories: 180 kcal, Fat: 4g (0.14 oz), Carbs: 32g (1.1 oz), Protein: 5g (0.18 oz), Sodium: 60mg, Potassium: 500mg, Phosphorus: 100mg

Storage: Store leftovers in an airtight container in the refrigerator for up to 3 days.

Presentation: Serve in bowls garnished with a sprig of thyme.

Variations: Add a pinch of nutmeg for extra warmth.

181. TOMATO AND LENTIL SOUP

Preparation Time: 15 minutes
Cooking Time: 40 minutes
Servings: 4

Ingredients:
- Red lentils: 1 cup (200g / 7 oz)
- Tomatoes, diced: 4 (400g / 14 oz)
- Carrot, diced: 1 (100g / 3.5 oz)
- Onion, diced: 1 (100g / 3.5 oz)
- Low-sodium vegetable broth: 6 cups (1.5 litres / 50 fl oz)
- Ground cumin: 1 tsp (2g / 0.07 oz)
- Black pepper: 1/4 tsp (0.5g / 0.02 oz)
- Fresh coriander, chopped: 2 tbsp (6g / 0.21 oz)

Directions:
Rinse the lentils under cold water.
In a large pot, combine all ingredients except coriander.
Bring to a boil, then reduce heat and simmer for 40 minutes, until lentils and vegetables are tender.
Puree with an immersion blender until smooth.
Season with black pepper and garnish with fresh coriander before serving.

Nutritional Information (per serving):
Calories: 220 kcal, Fat: 2g (0.07 oz), Carbs: 40g (1.4 oz), Protein: 12g (0.42 oz), Sodium: 50mg, Potassium: 600mg, Phosphorus: 200mg

Storage: Store leftovers in an airtight container in the refrigerator for up to 3 days.

Presentation: Serve in bowls garnished with a sprinkle of coriander.

Variations: Add a pinch of chili powder for a spicy kick.

182. CARROT AND GINGER SOUP

Preparation Time: 15 minutes
Cooking Time: 30 minutes
Servings: 4

Ingredients:
- Carrots, diced: 6 (600g / 1.3 lb)
- Fresh ginger, grated: 1 tbsp (6g / 0.21 oz)
- Onion, diced: 1 (100g / 3.5 oz)
- Low-sodium vegetable broth: 6 cups (1.5 litres / 50 fl oz)
- Fresh coriander, chopped: 2 tbsp (6g / 0.21 oz)
- Black pepper: 1/4 tsp (0.5g / 0.02 oz)

Directions:
In a large pot, sauté the onion and ginger until softened.
Add the carrots and vegetable broth.
Bring to a boil, then reduce heat and simmer for 25 minutes.
Puree with an immersion blender until smooth.
Season with black pepper and garnish with fresh coriander before serving.

Nutritional Information (per serving):
Calories: 160 kcal, Fat: 1g (0.04 oz), Carbs: 36g (1.3 oz), Protein: 3g (0.11 oz), Sodium: 50mg, Potassium: 700mg, Phosphorus: 90mg

Storage: Store leftovers in an airtight container in the refrigerator for up to 3 days.

Presentation: Serve in bowls garnished with a sprinkle of coriander.

Variations: Add a dash of orange juice for a citrus twist.

183. LEEK AND SPINACH SOUP

Preparation Time: 15 minutes
Cooking Time: 30 minutes
Servings: 4

Ingredients:
- Leeks, sliced: 4 (400g / 14 oz)
- Freshspinach: 4 cups (120g / 4.2 oz)
- Potato, peeled and diced: 1 (150g / 5.3 oz)
- Low-sodium vegetable broth: 6 cups (1.5 litres / 50 fl oz)
- Black pepper: 1/4 tsp (0.5g / 0.02 oz)
- Fresh parsley, chopped: 2 tbsp (6g / 0.21 oz)

Directions:
In a large pot, sauté the leeks until softened.
Add the potato and vegetable broth.
Bring to a boil, then reduce heat and simmer for 25 minutes.
Add the spinach and cook until wilted.
Puree with an immersion blender until smooth.
Season with black pepper and garnish with fresh parsley before serving.

Nutritional Information (per serving):
Calories: 150 kcal, Fat: 1g (0.04 oz), Carbs: 30g (1.1 oz), Protein: 4g (0.14 oz), Sodium: 40mg, Potassium: 600mg, Phosphorus: 100mg

Storage: Store leftovers in an airtight container in the refrigerator for up to 3 days.

Presentation: Serve in bowls garnished with a sprinkle of parsley.

Variations: Add a handful of kale for extra greens.

184. CREAMY CELERY SOUP

Preparation Time: 15 minutes
Cooking Time: 30 minutes
Servings: 4

Ingredients:
- Celery, diced: 6 stalks (300g / 10.5 oz)
- Potato, peeled and diced: 1 (150g / 5.3 oz)
- Onion, diced: 1 (100g / 3.5 oz)
- Low-sodium vegetable broth: 6 cups (1.5 litres / 50 fl oz)
- Low-fat milk: 1 cup (240ml / 8 oz)
- Black pepper: 1/4 tsp (0.5g / 0.02 oz)
- Fresh parsley, chopped: 2 tbsp (6g / 0.21 oz)

Directions:
In a large pot, sauté the onion and celery until softened.
Add the potato and vegetable broth.
Bring to a boil, then reduce heat and simmer for 25 minutes.
Puree with an immersion blender until smooth.
Stir in the milk and season with black pepper.
Garnish with fresh parsley before serving.

Nutritional Information (per serving):
Calories: 140 kcal, Fat: 2g (0.07 oz), Carbs: 26g (0.9 oz), Protein: 5g (0.18 oz), Sodium: 50mg, Potassium: 500mg, Phosphorus: 100mg

Storage: Store leftovers in an airtight container in the refrigerator for up to 3 days.

Presentation: Serve in bowls garnished with a sprinkle of parsley.

Variations: Add a handful of spinach for extra greens.

185. PUMPKIN AND SAGE SOUP

Preparation Time: 15 minutes
Cooking Time: 30 minutes
Servings: 4

Ingredients:
- Pumpkin, peeled and diced: 4 cups (600g / 1.3 lb)
- Onion, diced: 1 (100g / 3.5 oz)
- Fresh sage leaves, chopped: 1 tbsp (3g / 0.1 oz)
- Low-sodium vegetable broth: 6 cups (1.5 litres / 50 fl oz)
- Black pepper: 1/4 tsp (0.5g / 0.02 oz)
- Low-fat milk: 1 cup (240ml / 8 oz)

Directions:
In a large pot, sauté the onion and sage until softened.
Add the pumpkin and vegetable broth.
Bring to a boil, then reduce heat and simmer for 25 minutes.
Puree with an immersion blender until smooth.
Stir in the milk and season with black pepper.

Nutritional Information (per serving):
Calories: 180 kcal, Fat: 2g (0.07 oz), Carbs: 36g (1.3 oz), Protein: 5g (0.18 oz), Sodium: 50mg, Potassium: 700mg, Phosphorus: 100mg

Storage: Store leftovers in an airtight container in the refrigerator for up to 3 days.

Presentation: Serve in bowls garnished with a sprinkle of sage.

Variations: Add a pinch of nutmeg for extra warmth.

Chapter 7: Sweets and Snacks

BAKED SWEETS

186. APPLE AND CINNAMON MUFFINS

Preparation Time: 15 minutes
Cooking Time: 25 minutes
Servings: 12 muffins

Ingredients:
- All-purpose flour: 2 cups (240g / 8.5 oz)
- Baking powder: 2 tsp (10g / 0.35 oz)
- Ground cinnamon: 1 tsp (2.5g / 0.09 oz)
- Unsalted butter, melted: 1/2 cup (120ml / 4 oz)
- Granulated sugar: 1/2 cup (100g / 3.5 oz)
- Eggs: 2 large
- Low-fat milk: 1 cup (240ml / 8 oz)
- Apples, peeled and diced: 1 cup (150g / 5.3 oz)

Directions:
Introduction: These apple and cinnamon muffins are a delightful treat, perfect for a sweet breakfast or an afternoon snack. They are low in sodium, making them kidney-friendly.
Preparation of Ingredients: Preheat your oven to 375°F (190°C). Line a muffin tin with paper liners.
Mixing the Batter: In a large bowl, combine the flour, baking powder, and cinnamon. In a separate bowl, whisk together the melted butter, sugar, eggs, and milk. Gradually add the wet ingredients to the dry ingredients, mixing until just combined. Fold in the diced apples.
Baking: Divide the batter evenly among the muffin cups. Bake for 20-25 minutes or until a toothpick inserted into the center of a muffin comes out clean.
Cooling: Allow the muffins to cool in the tin for 5 minutes before transferring them to a wire rack to cool completely.

Nutritional Information (per serving):
Calories: 180 kcal, Fat: 6g (0.21 oz), Carbs: 29g (1.02 oz), Protein: 3g (0.11 oz), Sodium: 50mg, Potassium: 70mg, Phosphorus: 50mg

Storage: Store in an airtight container at room temperature for up to 3 days or freeze for up to 3 months.

Presentation: Serve these muffins warm, perhaps with a dollop of low-fat Greek yogurt or a sprinkle of extra cinnamon on top.

Variations: Substitute apples with pears or berries for a different flavor. Use almond milk for a dairy-free option.

187. LEMON BLUEBERRY SCONES

Preparation Time: 15 minutes
Cooking Time: 20 minutes
Servings: 8

Ingredients:
- All-purpose flour: 2 cups (240g / 8.5 oz)
- Baking powder: 2 tsp (10g / 0.35 oz)
- Unsalted butter, cold and cubed: 1/2 cup (120g / 4 oz)
- Granulated sugar: 1/4 cup (50g / 1.75 oz)
- Lemon zest: 1 tbsp (6g / 0.21 oz)
- Fresh blueberries: 1 cup (150g / 5.3 oz)

- Low-fat milk: 1/2 cup (120ml / 4 oz)
- Egg: 1 large, beaten

Directions:
Introduction: These lemon blueberry scones are bursting with flavor and perfect for a light, kidney-friendly snack or breakfast.
Preparation of Ingredients: Preheat your oven to 400°F (200°C). Line a baking sheet with parchment paper.
Mixing the Dough: In a large bowl, combine the flour and baking powder. Cut in the cold butter until the mixture resembles coarse crumbs. Stir in the sugar, lemon zest, and blueberries.
Forming the Scones: Add the milk and beaten egg to the dry ingredients, mixing until just combined. Turn the dough onto a lightly floured surface and gently knead it a few times. Shape into a circle about 1 inch thick and cut into 8 wedges.
Baking: Place the wedges on the prepared baking sheet and bake for 15-20 minutes, or until golden brown.

Nutritional Information (per serving):
Calories: 220 kcal, Fat: 9g (0.32 oz), Carbs: 30g (1.06 oz), Protein: 4g (0.14 oz), Sodium: 80mg, Potassium: 70mg, Phosphorus: 60mg

Storage: Store in an airtight container at room temperature for up to 3 days or freeze for up to 3 months.
Presentation: Serve the scones warm with a side of low-fat yogurt or a drizzle of honey. Garnish with extra lemon zest for a fresh look.
Variations: Substitute blueberries with raspberries or blackberries. For a dairy-free option, use almond milk and dairy-free butter.

188. RASPBERRY OAT BARS

Preparation Time: 15 minutes
Cooking Time: 35 minutes
Servings: 16 bars

Ingredients:
- Rolled oats: 1 1/2 cups (135g / 4.8 oz)
- All-purpose flour: 1 cup (120g / 4.2 oz)
- Brown sugar: 1/2 cup (100g / 3.5 oz)
- Unsalted butter, melted: 1/2 cup (120ml / 4 oz)
- Fresh raspberries: 2 cups (300g / 10.6 oz)
- Lemon juice: 1 tbsp (15ml / 0.5 oz)
- Honey: 1/4 cup (60ml / 2 oz)

Directions:
Introduction: These raspberry oat bars are a perfect combination of sweet and tart, making them a delicious and kidney-friendly snack.
Preparation of Ingredients: Preheat your oven to 350°F (175°C). Line an 8x8 inch baking pan with parchment paper.
Making the Crust and Topping: In a large bowl, combine the oats, flour, and brown sugar. Stir in the melted butter until the mixture is crumbly. Reserve 1/2 cup of this mixture for the topping and press the rest into the bottom of the prepared pan.
Preparing the Filling: In a separate bowl, mix the raspberries, lemon juice, and honey. Spread this mixture evenly over the crust.
Baking: Sprinkle the reserved oat mixture over the raspberry layer. Bake for 30-35 minutes, or until the top is golden brown.
Cooling: Allow to cool completely in the pan before cutting into bars.

Nutritional Information (per serving):
Calories: 180 kcal, Fat: 6g (0.21 oz), Carbs: 30g (1.06 oz), Protein: 2g (0.07 oz), Sodium: 20mg, Potassium: 70mg, Phosphorus: 50mg

Storage: Store in an airtight container at room

temperature for up to 3 days or refrigerate for up to a week.

Presentation: Serve these bars on a platter, garnished with fresh raspberries for an appealing presentation.

Variations: Substitute raspberries with strawberries or blueberries for a different flavor.

189. PEAR AND GINGER LOAF

Preparation Time: 15 minutes
Cooking Time: 50 minutes
Servings: 8

Ingredients:
- All-purpose flour: 2 cups (240g / 8.5 oz)
- Baking powder: 2 tsp (10g / 0.35 oz)
- Ground ginger: 1 tsp (2.5g / 0.09 oz)
- Unsalted butter, melted: 1/2 cup (120ml / 4 oz)
- Granulated sugar: 1/2 cup (100g / 3.5 oz)
- Eggs: 2 large
- Low-fat milk: 1/2 cup (120ml / 4 oz)
- Pears, peeled and diced: 1 cup (150g / 5.3 oz)

Directions:

Introduction: This pear and ginger loaf is a moist and flavorful treat, perfect for a kidney-friendly dessert or snack.

Preparation of Ingredients: Preheat your oven to 350°F (175°C). Grease a 9x5 inch loaf pan or line it with parchment paper.

Mixing the Batter: In a large bowl, combine the flour, baking powder, and ginger. In a separate bowl, whisk together the melted butter, sugar, eggs, and milk. Gradually add the wet ingredients to the dry ingredients, mixing until just combined. Fold in the diced pears.

Baking: Pour the batter into the prepared loaf pan. Bake for 50-55 minutes or until a toothpick inserted into the center comes out clean.

Cooling: Allow the loaf to cool in the pan for 10 minutes before transferring it to a wire rack to cool completely.

Nutritional Information (per serving):
Calories: 220 kcal, Fat: 8g (0.28 oz), Carbs: 35g (1.23 oz), Protein: 4g (0.14 oz), Sodium: 50mg, Potassium: 80mg, Phosphorus: 60mg

Storage: Store in an airtight container at room temperature for up to 3 days or freeze for up to 3 months.

Presentation: Slice the loaf and arrange it on a serving platter. Garnish with thin slices of fresh pear and a sprinkle of ground ginger.

Variations: Use apples instead of pears for a different flavor. Add a teaspoon of cinnamon for an extra spice kick.

190. BANANA BREAD

Preparation Time: 15 minutes
Cooking Time: 60 minutes
Servings: 10

Ingredients:
- All-purpose flour: 2 cups (240g / 8.5 oz)
- Baking soda: 1 tsp (5g / 0.18 oz)
- Ground cinnamon: 1 tsp (2.5g / 0.09 oz)
- Unsalted butter, melted: 1/2 cup (120ml / 4 oz)
- Granulated sugar: 1/2 cup (100g / 3.5 oz)
- Eggs: 2 large
- Overripe bananas, mashed: 1 cup (240g / 8.5 oz)
- Low-fat milk: 1/4 cup (60ml / 2 oz)
- Vanilla extract: 1 tsp (5ml / 0.18 oz)

Directions:

Introduction: This classic banana bread is moist and flavorful, perfect for a kidney-friendly snack or dessert.

Preparation of Ingredients: Preheat your oven to 350°F (175°C). Grease a 9x5 inch loaf pan or line it with parchment paper.

Mixing the Batter: In a large bowl, combine the flour, baking soda, and cinnamon. In a separate bowl, whisk together the melted butter, sugar, eggs, mashed bananas, milk, and vanilla extract. Gradually add the wet ingredients to the dry ingredients, mixing until just combined.

Baking: Pour the batter into the prepared loaf pan. Bake for 60-65 minutes or until a toothpick inserted into the center comes out clean.

Cooling: Allow the bread to cool in the pan for 10 minutes before transferring it to a wire rack to cool completely.

Nutritional Information (per serving):
Calories: 200 kcal, Fat: 7g (0.25 oz), Carbs: 32g (1.13 oz), Protein: 3g (0.11 oz), Sodium: 50mg, Potassium: 100mg, Phosphorus: 50mg

Storage: Store in an airtight container at room temperature for up to 3 days or freeze for up to 3 months.

Presentation: Slice the banana bread and arrange it on a serving platter. Garnish with slices of fresh banana or a sprinkle of cinnamon.

Variations: Add 1/2 cup of chopped walnuts or chocolate chips for extra texture and flavor.

191. ALMOND BISCOTTI

Preparation Time: 15 minutes
Cooking Time: 45 minutes
Servings: 24 biscotti

Ingredients:

- All-purpose flour: 2 cups (240g / 8.5 oz)
- Baking powder: 1 tsp (5g / 0.18 oz)
- Granulated sugar: 3/4 cup (150g / 5.3 oz)
- Unsalted butter, softened: 1/4 cup (60g / 2 oz)
- Eggs: 2 large
- Almond extract: 1 tsp (5ml / 0.18 oz)
- Sliced almonds: 1 cup (150g / 5.3 oz)

Directions:

Introduction: These almond biscotti are crisp and perfect for dunking in tea or coffee. They are low in sodium, making them a kidney-friendly treat.

Preparation of Ingredients: Preheat your oven to 350°F (175°C). Line a baking sheet with parchment paper.

Mixing the Dough: In a large bowl, combine the flour and baking powder. In a separate bowl, beat together the sugar, butter, eggs, and almond extract until creamy. Gradually add the wet ingredients to the dry ingredients, mixing until just combined. Fold in the sliced almonds.

Baking the Biscotti: Divide the dough in half and shape each half into a log about 12 inches long and 2 inches wide. Place the logs on the prepared baking sheet and bake for 25-30 minutes, or until golden brown.

Cooling and Slicing: Allow the logs to cool for 10 minutes, then slice them diagonally into 1/2-inch-thick slices. Place the slices cut-side down on the baking sheet and bake for an additional 10-15 minutes, or until crisp.

Cooling: Allow the biscotti to cool completely on a wire rack before serving.

Nutritional Information (per serving):
Calories: 80 kcal, Fat: 3g (0.11 oz), Carbs: 12g (0.42 oz), Protein: 2g (0.07 oz), Sodium: 20mg, Potassium: 30mg, Phosphorus: 20mg

Storage: Store in an airtight container at room temperature for up to 2 weeks.

Presentation: Serve the biscotti in a decorative tin or jar. For a festive touch, drizzle with melted dark chocolate.

Variations: Substitute almonds with hazelnuts or pistachios. Add 1/4 cup of dried cranberries for a fruity twist.

192. CARROT CAKE SQUARES

Preparation Time: 20 minutes
Cooking Time: 30 minutes
Servings: 16 squares

Ingredients:

- All-purpose flour: 1 1/2 cups (180g / 6.35 oz)
- Baking soda: 1 tsp (5g / 0.18 oz)
- Ground cinnamon: 1 tsp (2.5g / 0.09 oz)
- Ground nutmeg: 1/2 tsp (1.25g / 0.04 oz)
- Unsalted butter, melted: 1/2 cup (120ml / 4 oz)
- Brown sugar: 3/4 cup (150g / 5.3 oz)
- Eggs: 2 large
- Grated carrots: 1 cup (240g / 8.5 oz)
- Low-fat yogurt: 1/2 cup (120ml / 4 oz)
- Vanilla extract: 1 tsp (5ml / 0.18 oz)

Directions:

Introduction: These carrot cake squares are moist and delicious, perfect for a kidney-friendly dessert or snack.

Preparation of Ingredients: Preheat your oven to 350°F (175°C). Grease a 9x9 inch baking pan or line it with parchment paper.

Mixing the Batter: In a large bowl, combine the flour, baking soda, cinnamon, and nutmeg. In a separate bowl, whisk together the melted butter, brown sugar, eggs, grated carrots, yogurt, and vanilla extract. Gradually add the wet ingredients to the dry ingredients, mixing until just combined.

Baking: Pour the batter into the prepared baking pan. Bake for 25-30 minutes or until a toothpick inserted into the center comes out clean.

Cooling: Allow the cake to cool in the pan for 10 minutes before transferring it to a wire rack to cool completely. Cut into squares.

Nutritional Information (per serving):
Calories: 150 kcal, Fat: 6g (0.21 oz), Carbs: 22g (0.78 oz), Protein: 2g (0.07 oz), Sodium: 70mg, Potassium: 80mg, Phosphorus: 40mg

Storage: Store in an airtight container at room temperature for up to 3 days or refrigerate for up to a week.

Presentation: Arrange the carrot cake squares on a platter and dust with a light sprinkle of powdered sugar. Garnish with grated carrots for a decorative touch.

Variations: Add 1/4 cup of raisins or chopped walnuts for extra texture. Use coconut yogurt for a dairy-free version.

CAKES

193. CLASSIC VICTORIA SPONGE CAKE

Preparation Time: 20 minutes
Cooking Time: 25 minutes
Servings: 12

Ingredients:

- Self-raising flour: 1 1/2 cups (180g / 6.35 oz)
- Unsalted butter, softened: 3/4 cup (170g / 6 oz)
- Granulated sugar: 3/4 cup (150g / 5.3 oz)
- Eggs: 3 large
- Low-fat milk: 1/4 cup (60ml / 2 oz)

- Vanilla extract: 1 tsp (5ml / 0.18 oz)
- Strawberry jam: 1/2 cup (120g / 4 oz)
- Whipped cream: 1 cup (240ml / 8 oz)

Directions:
Introduction: This classic Victoria sponge cake is light and fluffy, perfect for a kidney-friendly dessert.

Preparation of Ingredients: Preheat your oven to 350°F (175°C). Grease and line two 8-inch round cake pans with parchment paper.

Mixing the Batter: In a large bowl, cream together the softened butter and sugar until light and fluffy. Beat in the eggs, one at a time, then add the vanilla extract. Gradually fold in the flour and milk until just combined.

Baking: Divide the batter evenly between the prepared cake pans. Bake for 20-25 minutes or until a toothpick inserted into the center comes out clean.

Cooling and Assembling: Allow the cakes to cool in the pans for 10 minutes before transferring them to a wire rack to cool completely. Spread the strawberry jam on one cake layer, top with whipped cream, and place the second cake layer on top.

Nutritional Information (per serving):
Calories: 220 kcal, Fat: 12g (0.42 oz), Carbs: 25g (0.88 oz), Protein: 3g (0.11 oz), Sodium: 60mg, Potassium: 50mg, Phosphorus: 40mg

Storage: Store in an airtight container at room temperature for up to 2 days or refrigerate for up to a week.

Presentation: Dust the top of the cake with powdered sugar and garnish with fresh strawberries for an elegant look.

Variations: Substitute the strawberry jam with raspberry jam or lemon curd for different flavors.

194. LEMON DRIZZLE CAKE

Preparation Time: 15 minutes
Cooking Time: 40 minutes
Servings: 10

Ingredients:
- All-purpose flour: 1 1/2 cups (180g / 6.35 oz)
- Baking powder: 1 tsp (5g / 0.18 oz)
- Unsalted butter, softened: 3/4 cup (170g / 6 oz)
- Granulated sugar: 3/4 cup (150g / 5.3 oz)
- Eggs: 3 large
- Low-fat milk: 1/4 cup (60ml / 2 oz)
- Lemon zest: 1 tbsp (6g / 0.21 oz)
- Lemon juice: 1/4 cup (60ml / 2 oz)
- Powdered sugar: 1/2 cup (60g / 2.1 oz)

Directions:
Introduction: This lemon drizzle cake is moist and tangy, perfect for a refreshing, kidney-friendly dessert.

Preparation of Ingredients: Preheat your oven to 350°F (175°C). Grease and line a 9x5 inch loaf pan with parchment paper.

Mixing the Batter: In a large bowl, cream together the softened butter and sugar until light and fluffy. Beat in the eggs, one at a time, then add the lemon zest and juice. Gradually fold in the flour, baking powder, and milk until just combined.

Baking: Pour the batter into the prepared loaf pan. Bake for 35-40 minutes or until a toothpick inserted into the center comes out clean.

Making the Drizzle: In a small bowl, mix the powdered sugar with 2 tablespoons of lemon juice until smooth. Pour over the warm cake and allow to cool completely in the pan.

Nutritional Information (per serving):

Calories: 220 kcal, Fat: 10g (0.35 oz), Carbs: 30g (1.06 oz), Protein: 3g (0.11 oz), Sodium: 60mg, Potassium: 50mg, Phosphorus: 40mg

Storage: Store in an airtight container at room temperature for up to 3 days or refrigerate for up to a week.

Presentation: Serve slices of the lemon drizzle cake on a platter, garnished with lemon zest for a bright, fresh look.

Variations: Add poppy seeds to the batter for a lemon poppy seed cake. Substitute lemon with lime for a different citrus flavor.

195. CHOCOLATE BEETROOT CAKE

Preparation Time: 20 minutes
Cooking Time: 35 minutes
Servings: 12

Ingredients:
- All-purpose flour: 1 1/2 cups (180g / 6.35 oz)
- Baking soda: 1 tsp (5g / 0.18 oz)
- Unsweetened cocoa powder: 1/2 cup (50g / 1.75 oz)
- Granulated sugar: 3/4 cup (150g / 5.3 oz)
- Unsalted butter, melted: 1/2 cup (120ml / 4 oz)
- Eggs: 3 large
- Grated beetroot: 1 cup (150g / 5.3 oz)
- Low-fat milk: 1/4 cup (60ml / 2 oz)
- Vanilla extract: 1 tsp (5ml / 0.18 oz)

Directions:
Introduction: This chocolate beetroot cake is rich and moist, perfect for a unique and kidney-friendly dessert.

Preparation of Ingredients: Preheat your oven to 350°F (175°C). Grease and line a 9-inch round cake pan with parchment paper.

Mixing the Batter: In a large bowl, combine the flour, baking soda, and cocoa powder. In a separate bowl, whisk together the melted butter, sugar, eggs, grated beetroot, milk, and vanilla extract. Gradually add the wet ingredients to the dry ingredients, mixing until just combined.

Baking: Pour the batter into the prepared cake pan. Bake for 30-35 minutes or until a toothpick inserted into the center comes out clean.

Cooling: Allow the cake to cool in the pan for 10 minutes before transferring it to a wire rack to cool completely.

Nutritional Information (per serving):
Calories: 200 kcal, Fat: 8g (0.28 oz), Carbs: 30g (1.06 oz), Protein: 3g (0.11 oz), Sodium: 50mg, Potassium: 100mg, Phosphorus: 60mg

Storage: Store in an airtight container at room temperature for up to 3 days or refrigerate for up to a week.

Presentation: Dust the top of the cake with powdered sugar and garnish with fresh beetroot shavings for a decorative touch.

Variations: Substitute beetroot with grated zucchini for a different vegetable-based cake.

196. ORANGE POLENTA CAKE

Preparation Time: 20 minutes
Cooking Time: 40 minutes
Servings: 10

Ingredients:
- Cornmeal (polenta): 1 cup (150g / 5.3 oz)
- All-purpose flour: 1 cup (120g / 4.2 oz)
- Baking powder: 1 tsp (5g / 0.18 oz)

- Unsalted butter, softened: 3/4 cup (170g / 6 oz)
- Granulated sugar: 3/4 cup (150g / 5.3 oz)
- Eggs: 3 large
- Orange zest: 1 tbsp (6g / 0.21 oz)
- Orange juice: 1/4 cup (60ml / 2 oz)
- Low-fat yogurt: 1/2 cup (120ml / 4 oz)

Directions:
Introduction: This orange polenta cake is moist and fragrant, perfect for a refreshing and kidney-friendly dessert.
Preparation of Ingredients: Preheat your oven to 350°F (175°C). Grease and line a 9-inch round cake pan with parchment paper.
Mixing the Batter: In a large bowl, combine the cornmeal, flour, and baking powder. In a separate bowl, cream together the softened butter and sugar until light and fluffy. Beat in the eggs, one at a time, then add the orange zest, juice, and yogurt. Gradually add the wet ingredients to the dry ingredients, mixing until just combined.
Baking: Pour the batter into the prepared cake pan. Bake for 35-40 minutes or until a toothpick inserted into the center comes out clean.
Cooling: Allow the cake to cool in the pan for 10 minutes before transferring it to a wire rack to cool completely.

Nutritional Information (per serving):
Calories: 220 kcal, Fat: 9g (0.32 oz), Carbs: 30g (1.06 oz), Protein: 4g (0.14 oz), Sodium: 50mg, Potassium: 70mg, Phosphorus: 60mg

Storage: Store in an airtight container at room temperature for up to 3 days or refrigerate for up to a week.

Presentation: Serve slices of the orange polenta cake on a platter, garnished with orange zest or thin slices of fresh orange.

Variations: Add a tablespoon of poppy seeds to the batter for extra texture. Substitute orange with lemon for a different citrus flavor.

197. COCONUT LIME CAKE

Preparation Time: 20 minutes
Cooking Time: 35 minutes
Servings: 12

Ingredients:
- All-purpose flour: 1 1/2 cups (180g / 6.35 oz)
- Baking powder: 1 tsp (5g / 0.18 oz)
- Unsalted butter, softened: 3/4 cup (170g / 6 oz)
- Granulated sugar: 3/4 cup (150g / 5.3 oz)
- Eggs: 3 large
- Low-fat milk: 1/4 cup (60ml / 2 oz)
- Lime zest: 1 tbsp (6g / 0.21 oz)
- Lime juice: 1/4 cup (60ml / 2 oz)
- Shredded coconut: 1 cup (150g / 5.3 oz)

Directions:
Introduction: This coconut lime cake is tropical and refreshing, perfect for a kidney-friendly dessert.
Preparation of Ingredients: Preheat your oven to 350°F (175°C). Grease and line a 9-inch round cake pan with parchment paper.
Mixing the Batter: In a large bowl, combine the flour and baking powder. In a separate bowl, cream together the softened butter and sugar until light and fluffy. Beat in the eggs, one at a time, then add the lime zest, juice, and milk. Gradually add the wet ingredients to the dry ingredients, mixing until just combined. Fold in the shredded coconut.
Baking: Pour the batter into the prepared cake pan. Bake for 30-35 minutes or until a toothpick inserted into the center comes out clean.

Cooling: Allow the cake to cool in the pan for 10 minutes before transferring it to a wire rack to cool completely.

Nutritional Information (per serving):
Calories: 230 kcal, Fat: 12g (0.42 oz), Carbs: 28g (0.99 oz), Protein: 3g (0.11 oz), Sodium: 50mg, Potassium: 70mg, Phosphorus: 50mg

Storage: Store in an airtight container at room temperature for up to 3 days or refrigerate for up to a week.

Presentation: Garnish the cake with extra shredded coconut and lime zest. Serve slices with a dollop of whipped cream or a scoop of low-fat yogurt.

Variations: Substitute lime with lemon or orange for a different citrus flavor. Add a handful of chopped nuts for extra texture.

198. BERRY YOGURT CAKE

Preparation Time: 20 minutes
Cooking Time: 35 minutes
Servings: 12

Ingredients:
- All-purpose flour: 1 1/2 cups (180g / 6.35 oz)
- Baking powder: 1 tsp (5g / 0.18 oz)
- Unsalted butter, softened: 3/4 cup (170g / 6 oz)
- Granulated sugar: 3/4 cup (150g / 5.3 oz)
- Eggs: 3 large
- Low-fat yogurt: 1/2 cup (120ml / 4 oz)
- Vanilla extract: 1 tsp (5ml / 0.18 oz)
- Mixed berries (fresh or frozen): 1 cup (150g / 5.3 oz)

Directions:
Introduction: This berry yogurt cake is light and fruity, perfect for a refreshing and kidney-friendly dessert.

Preparation of Ingredients: Preheat your oven to 350°F (175°C). Grease and line a 9-inch round cake pan with parchment paper.

Mixing the Batter: In a large bowl, combine the flour and baking powder. In a separate bowl, cream together the softened butter and sugar until light and fluffy. Beat in the eggs, one at a time, then add the yogurt and vanilla extract. Gradually add the wet ingredients to the dry ingredients, mixing until just combined. Fold in the mixed berries.

Baking: Pour the batter into the prepared cake pan. Bake for 30-35 minutes or until a toothpick inserted into the center comes out clean.

Cooling: Allow the cake to cool in the pan for 10 minutes before transferring it to a wire rack to cool completely.

Nutritional Information (per serving):
Calories: 210 kcal, Fat: 9g (0.32 oz), Carbs: 30g (1.06 oz), Protein: 4g (0.14 oz), Sodium: 50mg, Potassium: 70mg, Phosphorus: 50mg

Storage: Store in an airtight container at room temperature for up to 3 days or refrigerate for up to a week.

Presentation: Garnish the cake with extra berries and a dusting of powdered sugar. Serve slices with a dollop of whipped cream or a scoop of low-fat yogurt.

Variations: Use different combinations of berries for a variety of flavors. Substitute yogurt with sour cream for a richer texture.

199. GINGERBREAD CAKE

Preparation Time: 20 minutes
Cooking Time: 35 minutes
Servings: 12

Ingredients:

- All-purpose flour: 1 1/2 cups (180g / 6.35 oz)
- Baking soda: 1 tsp (5g / 0.18 oz)
- Ground ginger: 1 tsp (2.5g / 0.09 oz)
- Ground cinnamon: 1 tsp (2.5g / 0.09 oz)
- Unsalted butter, melted: 1/2 cup (120ml / 4 oz)
- Brown sugar: 1/2 cup (100g / 3.5 oz)
- Molasses: 1/2 cup (120ml / 4 oz)
- Eggs: 2 large
- Low-fat milk: 1/2 cup (120ml / 4 oz)

Directions:

Introduction: This gingerbread cake is rich and spicy, perfect for a cozy and kidney-friendly dessert.

Preparation of Ingredients: Preheat your oven to 350°F (175°C). Grease and line a 9-inch square baking pan with parchment paper.

Mixing the Batter: In a large bowl, combine the flour, baking soda, ginger, and cinnamon. In a separate bowl, whisk together the melted butter, brown sugar, molasses, eggs, and milk. Gradually add the wet ingredients to the dry ingredients, mixing until just combined.

Baking: Pour the batter into the prepared baking pan. Bake for 30-35 minutes or until a toothpick inserted into the center comes out clean.

Cooling: Allow the cake to cool in the pan for 10 minutes before transferring it to a wire rack to cool completely.

Nutritional Information (per serving):
Calories: 220 kcal, Fat: 8g (0.28 oz), Carbs: 34g (1.2 oz), Protein: 3g (0.11 oz), Sodium: 60mg, Potassium: 80mg, Phosphorus: 50mg

Storage: Store in an airtight container at room temperature for up to 3 days or refrigerate for up to a week.

Presentation: Dust the top of the gingerbread cake with powdered sugar and garnish with fresh ginger slices for a decorative touch.

Variations: Add 1/2 cup of raisins or chopped nuts for extra texture. Serve with a dollop of whipped cream or a scoop of low-fat ice cream.

COOKIES

200. OATMEAL RAISIN COOKIES

Preparation Time: 15 minutes
Cooking Time: 12 minutes
Servings: 24 cookies

Ingredients:

- Rolled oats: 1 1/2 cups (135g / 4.8 oz)
- All-purpose flour: 1 cup (120g / 4.2 oz)
- Baking powder: 1 tsp (5g / 0.18 oz)
- Ground cinnamon: 1 tsp (2.5g / 0.09 oz)
- Unsalted butter, softened: 1/2 cup (120g / 4 oz)
- Brown sugar: 1/2 cup (100g / 3.5 oz)
- Granulated sugar: 1/4 cup (50g / 1.75 oz)
- Egg: 1 large
- Vanilla extract: 1 tsp (5ml / 0.18 oz)
- Raisins: 1 cup (150g / 5.3 oz)

Directions:

Introduction: These oatmeal raisin cookies are chewy and delicious, perfect for a kidney-friendly snack.

Preparation of Ingredients: Preheat your oven to 350°F (175°C). Line a baking sheet with parchment paper.

Mixing the Dough: In a large bowl, combine the oats, flour, baking powder, and cinnamon. In a separate bowl, cream together the softened butter, brown sugar, and granulated sugar until light and fluffy. Beat in the egg and vanilla extract. Gradually add the wet ingredients to the dry ingredients, mixing until just combined. Fold in the raisins.

Baking: Drop tablespoonfuls of dough onto the prepared baking sheet, spacing them about 2 inches apart. Bake for 10-12 minutes, or until the edges are golden brown.

Cooling: Allow the cookies to cool on the baking sheet for 5 minutes before transferring them to a wire rack to cool completely.

Nutritional Information (per serving):
Calories: 90 kcal, Fat: 3g (0.11 oz), Carbs: 15g (0.53 oz), Protein: 1g (0.04 oz), Sodium: 40mg, Potassium: 70mg, Phosphorus: 20mg

Storage: Store in an airtight container at room temperature for up to a week.

Presentation: Serve the cookies on a platter, perhaps with a side of cold milk or tea.

Variations: Substitute raisins with dried cranberries or chopped dried apricots. Add 1/2 cup of chopped nuts for extra texture.

201. CHOCOLATE CHIP COOKIES

Preparation Time: 15 minutes
Cooking Time: 12 minutes
Servings: 24 cookies

Ingredients:
- All-purpose flour: 1 1/2 cups (180g / 6.35 oz)
- Baking soda: 1 tsp (5g / 0.18 oz)
- Unsalted butter, softened: 1/2 cup (120g / 4 oz)
- Brown sugar: 1/2 cup (100g / 3.5 oz)
- Granulated sugar: 1/4 cup (50g / 1.75 oz)
- Egg: 1 large
- Vanilla extract: 1 tsp (5ml / 0.18 oz)
- Dark chocolate chips: 1 cup (150g / 5.3 oz)

Directions:

Introduction: These chocolate chip cookies are classic and delicious, perfect for a kidney-friendly treat.

Preparation of Ingredients: Preheat your oven to 350°F (175°C). Line a baking sheet with parchment paper.

Mixing the Dough: In a large bowl, combine the flour and baking soda. In a separate bowl, cream together the softened butter, brown sugar, and granulated sugar until light and fluffy. Beat in the egg and vanilla extract. Gradually add the wet ingredients to the dry ingredients, mixing until just combined. Fold in the chocolate chips.

Baking: Drop tablespoonfuls of dough onto the prepared baking sheet, spacing them about 2 inches apart. Bake for 10-12 minutes, or until the edges are golden brown.

Cooling: Allow the cookies to cool on the baking sheet for 5 minutes before transferring them to a wire rack to cool completely.

Nutritional Information (per serving):
Calories: 100 kcal, Fat: 4g (0.14 oz), Carbs: 15g (0.53 oz), Protein: 1g (0.04 oz), Sodium: 40mg, Potassium: 50mg, Phosphorus: 20mg

Storage: Store in an airtight container at room temperature for up to a week.

Presentation: Serve the cookies on a platter, perhaps with a side of cold milk or hot coffee.

Variations: Substitute dark chocolate chips with white chocolate or milk chocolate chips. Add 1/2 cup of chopped nuts for extra texture.

202. LEMON SUGAR COOKIES

Preparation Time: 15 minutes
Cooking Time: 10 minutes
Servings: 24 cookies

Ingredients:
- All-purpose flour: 1 1/2 cups (180g / 6.35 oz)
- Baking powder: 1 tsp (5g / 0.18 oz)
- Unsalted butter, softened: 1/2 cup (120g / 4 oz)
- Granulated sugar: 1/2 cup (100g / 3.5 oz)
- Egg: 1 large
- Lemon zest: 1 tbsp (6g / 0.21 oz)
- Lemon juice: 2 tbsp (30ml / 1 oz)

Directions:
Introduction: These lemon sugar cookies are light and zesty, perfect for a refreshing, kidney-friendly snack.
Preparation of Ingredients: Preheat your oven to 350°F (175°C). Line a baking sheet with parchment paper.
Mixing the Dough: In a large bowl, combine the flour and baking powder. In a separate bowl, cream together the softened butter and sugar until light and fluffy. Beat in the egg, lemon zest, and lemon juice. Gradually add the wet ingredients to the dry ingredients, mixing until just combined.
Baking: Drop tablespoonfuls of dough onto the prepared baking sheet, spacing them about 2 inches apart. Bake for 8-10 minutes, or until the edges are golden brown.
Cooling: Allow the cookies to cool on the baking sheet for 5 minutes before transferring them to a wire rack to cool completely.

Nutritional Information (per serving):
Calories: 80 kcal, Fat: 3g (0.11 oz), Carbs: 12g (0.42 oz), Protein: 1g (0.04 oz), Sodium: 30mg, Potassium: 30mg, Phosphorus: 10mg

Storage: Store in an airtight container at room temperature for up to a week.

Presentation: Serve the cookies on a decorative plate, garnished with lemon slices or zest.

Variations: Add a tablespoon of poppy seeds to the dough for a lemon poppy seed cookie. Substitute lemon with lime or orange for different citrus flavors.

203. PEANUT BUTTER COOKIES

Preparation Time: 15 minutes
Cooking Time: 12 minutes
Servings: 24 cookies

Ingredients:
- All-purpose flour: 1 cup (120g / 4.2 oz)
- Baking powder: 1 tsp (5g / 0.18 oz)
- Unsalted butter, softened: 1/2 cup (120g / 4 oz)
- Brown sugar: 1/2 cup (100g / 3.5 oz)
- Creamy peanut butter: 1/2 cup (120g / 4 oz)
- Egg: 1 large
- Vanilla extract: 1 tsp (5ml / 0.18 oz)

Directions:
Introduction: These peanut butter cookies are rich and delicious, perfect for a kidney-friendly snack.
Preparation of Ingredients: Preheat your oven to 350°F (175°C). Line a baking sheet with parchment paper.
Mixing the Dough: In a large bowl, combine the flour and baking powder. In a separate bowl, cream together the softened butter, brown sugar, and peanut butter until light and fluffy. Beat in the egg

and vanilla extract. Gradually add the wet ingredients to the dry ingredients, mixing until just combined.

Baking: Drop tablespoonfuls of dough onto the prepared baking sheet, spacing them about 2 inches apart. Flatten each cookie with a fork, making a crisscross pattern. Bake for 10-12 minutes, or until the edges are golden brown.

Cooling: Allow the cookies to cool on the baking sheet for 5 minutes before transferring them to a wire rack to cool completely.

Nutritional Information (per serving):
Calories: 100 kcal, Fat: 6g (0.21 oz), Carbs: 10g (0.35 oz), Protein: 2g (0.07 oz), Sodium: 50mg, Potassium: 70mg, Phosphorus: 30mg

Storage: Store in an airtight container at room temperature for up to a week.

Presentation: Serve the cookies on a plate, garnished with a few whole peanuts or a drizzle of melted chocolate.

Variations: Add 1/2 cup of chocolate chips to the dough for chocolate peanut butter cookies. Substitute peanut butter with almond butter for a different flavor.

204. ALMOND BISCOTTI

Preparation Time: 20 minutes
Cooking Time: 45 minutes
Servings: 24 cookies

Ingredients:

- All-purpose flour: 2 cups (240g / 8.5 oz)
- Baking powder: 1 tsp (5g / 0.18 oz)
- Granulated sugar: 3/4 cup (150g / 5.3 oz)
- Unsalted butter, softened: 1/4 cup (60g / 2 oz)
- Eggs: 2 large
- Almond extract: 1 tsp (5ml / 0.18 oz)
- Sliced almonds: 1 cup (150g / 5.3 oz)

Directions:

Introduction: These almond biscotti are crisp and perfect for dunking in tea or coffee. They are low in sodium, making them a kidney-friendly treat.

Preparation of Ingredients: Preheat your oven to 350°F (175°C). Line a baking sheet with parchment paper.

Mixing the Dough: In a large bowl, combine the flour and baking powder. In a separate bowl, beat together the sugar, butter, eggs, and almond extract until creamy. Gradually add the wet ingredients to the dry ingredients, mixing until just combined. Fold in the sliced almonds.

Baking the Biscotti: Divide the dough in half and shape each half into a log about 12 inches long and 2 inches wide. Place the logs on the prepared baking sheet and bake for 25-30 minutes, or until golden brown.

Cooling and Slicing: Allow the logs to cool for 10 minutes, then slice them diagonally into 1/2-inch-thick slices. Place the slices cut-side down on the baking sheet and bake for an additional 10-15 minutes, or until crisp.

Cooling: Allow the biscotti to cool completely on a wire rack before serving.

Nutritional Information (per serving):
Calories: 80 kcal, Fat: 3g (0.11 oz), Carbs: 12g (0.42 oz), Protein: 2g (0.07 oz), Sodium: 20mg, Potassium: 30mg, Phosphorus: 20mg

Storage: Store in an airtight container at room temperature for up to 2 weeks.

Presentation: Serve the biscotti in a decorative tin or jar. For a festive touch, drizzle with melted dark chocolate.

Variations: Substitute almonds with hazelnuts or pistachios. Add 1/4 cup of dried cranberries for a fruity twist.

SAVORY SNACKS

205. ROSEMARY CHICKPEA CRISPS

Preparation Time: 10 minutes
Cooking Time: 40 minutes
Servings: 4

Ingredients:
- Chickpeas, drained and dried: 2 cups (400g / 14 oz)
- Extra virgin olive oil: 2 tbsp (30ml / 1 oz)
- Fresh rosemary, finely chopped: 1 tbsp (1.5g / 0.05 oz)
- Freshly ground black pepper: 1/4 tsp (0.5g / 0.02 oz)
- Salt (optional, use sparingly to stay within 100 mg of sodium): a pinch

Directions:
Introduction: Rosemary Chickpea Crisps are the perfect snack for those looking for a crunchy and healthy alternative. Baked with olive oil, fresh rosemary, and a sprinkle of black pepper, these chickpeas offer a delightful flavor combination that satisfies the craving for something savory without compromising health.
Preparation of Ingredients: Begin by rinsing the chickpeas under cold water and thoroughly drying them with paper towels. It's crucial that they're completely dry to ensure maximum crispiness after baking.
Assemblage: Preheat the oven to 400°F (200°C). In a bowl, toss the dried chickpeas with olive oil, chopped rosemary, and freshly ground black pepper until evenly coated. If using, sprinkle a pinch of salt over the chickpeas.
Specific Cooking Times: Spread the chickpeas in a single layer on a baking sheet lined with parchment paper. Bake in the preheated oven for 40 minutes, or until they are golden and crispy. Shake the pan or stir the chickpeas halfway through baking to ensure they crisp up evenly.
Cooling and Resting: Allow the chickpea crisps to cool on the baking sheet for a few minutes before serving. They will continue to crisp up as they cool.
Cooking Tips: To achieve the best texture, make sure the chickpeas are thoroughly dried before seasoning and baking. Experiment with the baking time to find the perfect level of crispiness you prefer.

Nutritional Information (per serving):
Calories: 210 kcal, Fat: 8g (0.28 oz), Carbs: 28g (0.99 oz), Protein: 7g (0.25 oz), Sodium: 100mg (if salt is used sparingly)

Storage: Store any leftovers in an airtight container at room temperature for up to a week to maintain their crispness.

Presentation: Serve the chickpea crisps in a bowl or on a platter, garnished with additional rosemary sprigs for a touch of elegance and an indication of their flavor.

Variations: Feel free to experiment with other herbs and spices such as thyme, smoked paprika, or cumin for different flavor profiles.

206. BAKED ZUCCHINI CHIPS

Preparation Time: 10 minutes
Cooking Time: 25 minutes
Servings: 4

Ingredients:
- Zucchini, thinly sliced: 2 cups (300g / 10.6 oz)
- Olive oil: 1 tbsp (15ml / 0.5 oz)
- Garlic powder: 1/2 tsp (2.5g / 0.09 oz)

- Paprika: 1/2 tsp (2.5g / 0.09 oz)
- Freshly ground black pepper: 1/4 tsp (0.5g / 0.02 oz)
- Salt (optional, use sparingly to stay within 100 mg of sodium): a pinch

Directions:

Introduction: These baked zucchini chips are a healthy and flavorful alternative to traditional chips. Seasoned with garlic powder, paprika, and black pepper, they offer a satisfying crunch without excessive sodium.

Preparation of Ingredients: Preheat your oven to 425°F (220°C). Line a baking sheet with parchment paper.

Mixing the Seasoning: In a bowl, toss the thinly sliced zucchini with olive oil, garlic powder, paprika, and black pepper until evenly coated. If using, sprinkle a pinch of salt over the zucchini slices.

Baking: Arrange the zucchini slices in a single layer on the prepared baking sheet. Bake for 20-25 minutes, or until the chips are golden and crispy. Flip the slices halfway through baking to ensure even crispiness.

Cooling: Allow the zucchini chips to cool on the baking sheet for a few minutes before serving. They will continue to crisp up as they cool.

Nutritional Information (per serving):
Calories: 50 kcal, Fat: 3g (0.11 oz), Carbs: 5g (0.18 oz), Protein: 1g (0.04 oz), Sodium: 50mg, Potassium: 150mg, Phosphorus: 20mg

Storage: Store any leftovers in an airtight container at room temperature for up to 3 days.

Presentation: Serve the zucchini chips in a bowl, garnished with a sprinkle of paprika and fresh parsley for a touch of color.

Variations: Substitute zucchini with yellow squash or eggplant for a different vegetable chip. Experiment with other seasonings such as cayenne pepper or Italian herbs.

207. SPICED SWEET POTATO WEDGES

Preparation Time: 10 minutes
Cooking Time: 25 minutes
Servings: 4

Ingredients:
- Sweet potatoes, cut into wedges: 2 cups (400g / 14 oz)
- Olive oil: 2 tbsp (30ml / 1 oz)
- Ground cumin: 1/2 tsp (2.5g / 0.09 oz)
- Smoked paprika: 1/2 tsp (2.5g / 0.09 oz)
- Freshly ground black pepper: 1/4 tsp (0.5g / 0.02 oz)
- Salt (optional, use sparingly to stay within 100 mg of sodium): a pinch

Directions:

Introduction: These spiced sweet potato wedges are a delicious and healthy savory snack. Seasoned with cumin and smoked paprika, they offer a flavorful kick without excessive sodium.

Preparation of Ingredients: Preheat your oven to 425°F (220°C). Line a baking sheet with parchment paper.

Mixing the Seasoning: In a bowl, toss the sweet potato wedges with olive oil, cumin, smoked paprika, and black pepper until evenly coated. If using, sprinkle a pinch of salt over the wedges.

Baking: Arrange the sweet potato wedges in a single layer on the prepared baking sheet. Bake for 20-25 minutes, or until the wedges are golden and crispy. Flip the wedges halfway through baking to ensure even crispiness.

Cooling: Allow the sweet potato wedges to cool on the baking sheet for a few minutes before serving. They will continue to crisp up as they cool.

Nutritional Information (per serving):

Calories: 120 kcal, Fat: 5g (0.18 oz), Carbs: 18g (0.63 oz), Protein: 1g (0.04 oz), Sodium: 50mg, Potassium: 300mg, Phosphorus: 30mg

Storage: Store any leftovers in an airtight container in the refrigerator for up to 3 days.

Presentation: Serve the sweet potato wedges on a platter, garnished with fresh cilantro and a wedge of lime for added freshness.

Variations: Substitute sweet potatoes with regular potatoes or butternut squash. Experiment with other seasonings such as chili powder or garlic powder.

208. HERB-CRUSTED CAULIFLOWER BITES

Preparation Time: 10 minutes
Cooking Time: 20 minutes
Servings: 4

Ingredients:
- Cauliflower florets: 2 cups (300g / 10.6 oz)
- Olive oil: 2 tbsp (30ml / 1 oz)
- Bread crumbs: 1/2 cup (60g / 2.1 oz)
- Grated Parmesan cheese: 1/4 cup (25g / 0.88 oz)
- Dried thyme: 1 tsp (2g / 0.07 oz)
- Dried oregano: 1 tsp (2g / 0.07 oz)
- Freshly ground black pepper: 1/4 tsp (0.5g / 0.02 oz)
- Salt (optional, use sparingly to stay within 100 mg of sodium): a pinch

Directions:
Introduction: These herb-crusted cauliflower bites are a savory and crunchy snack. Coated with bread crumbs, Parmesan cheese, and herbs, they offer a flavorful alternative to traditional snacks.

Preparation of Ingredients: Preheat your oven to 425°F (220°C). Line a baking sheet with parchment paper.

Mixing the Coating: In a bowl, combine the bread crumbs, Parmesan cheese, thyme, oregano, and black pepper. Toss the cauliflower florets with olive oil until evenly coated, then roll them in the bread crumb mixture until well coated.

Baking: Arrange the coated cauliflower florets in a single layer on the prepared baking sheet. Bake for 20 minutes, or until the bites are golden and crispy.

Cooling: Allow the cauliflower bites to cool on the baking sheet for a few minutes before serving.

Nutritional Information (per serving):
Calories: 100 kcal, Fat: 6g (0.21 oz), Carbs: 10g (0.35 oz), Protein: 3g (0.11 oz), Sodium: 70mg, Potassium: 150mg, Phosphorus: 40mg

Storage: Store any leftovers in an airtight container in the refrigerator for up to 3 days.

Presentation: Serve the cauliflower bites on a platter, garnished with fresh parsley and a side of low-sodium dipping sauce.

Variations: Substitute cauliflower with broccoli or Brussels sprouts. Experiment with other herbs and spices such as basil or paprika.

209. CHEESE AND CHIVE POPCORN

Preparation Time: 5 minutes
Cooking Time: 10 minutes
Servings: 4

Ingredients:
- Popcorn kernels: 1/2 cup (120g / 4.2 oz)
- Olive oil: 2 tbsp (30ml / 1 oz)

- Grated Parmesan cheese: 1/4 cup (25g / 0.88 oz)
- Fresh chives, finely chopped: 2 tbsp (6g / 0.21 oz)
- Freshly ground black pepper: 1/4 tsp (0.5g / 0.02 oz)
- Salt (optional, use sparingly to stay within 100 mg of sodium): a pinch

Directions:

Introduction: This cheese and chive popcorn is a savory and delicious snack. Seasoned with Parmesan cheese, fresh chives, and black pepper, it offers a flavorful twist on traditional popcorn.

Popping the Popcorn: Heat the olive oil in a large pot over medium heat. Add the popcorn kernels and cover the pot. Cook, shaking the pot occasionally, until the popping slows down, about 5 minutes.

Seasoning: Transfer the popped popcorn to a large bowl. Sprinkle with Parmesan cheese, fresh chives, and black pepper. Toss until evenly coated. If using, sprinkle a pinch of salt over the popcorn.

Nutritional Information (per serving):
Calories: 150 kcal, Fat: 7g (0.25 oz), Carbs: 18g (0.63 oz), Protein: 4g (0.14 oz), Sodium: 70mg, Potassium: 70mg, Phosphorus: 50mg

Storage: Store any leftovers in an airtight container at room temperature for up to 3 days.

Presentation: Serve the popcorn in a large bowl, garnished with extra chives for a touch of color.

Variations: Substitute Parmesan cheese with nutritional yeast for a dairy-free option. Add a pinch of cayenne pepper for a spicy kick.

Chapter 8: British Drinks for Renal Well-being

210. ENGLISH ELDERFLOWER SPRITZER

Preparation Time: 5 minutes
Servings: 1

Ingredients:
- Elderflower cordial: 2 tbsp (30ml / 1 oz)
- Sparkling water: 1 cup (240ml / 8.45 oz)
- Lemon slice: 1
- Ice cubes: as needed

Directions:
Introduction: A refreshing spritz with the delicate flavor of elderflower, perfect for a summer day.
Preparation: Fill a glass with ice cubes.
Mixing: Add elderflower cordial and top up with sparkling water.
Assemblage: Garnish with a lemon slice.

Nutritional Information (per serving):
Calories: 30 kcal, Fat: 0g, Carbs: 8g (0.28 oz), Protein: 0g, Sodium: 10mg, Potassium: 20mg, Phosphorus: 5mg

Storage: Best served immediately.

Presentation: Serve in a tall glass with a straw.

Variations: Add a few fresh mint leaves for an extra burst of flavor.

211. CUCUMBER MINT COOLER

Preparation Time: 5 minutes
Servings: 1

Ingredients:
- Cucumber, sliced: 4-5 slices
- Fresh mint leaves: 5-6
- Lime juice: 1 tbsp (15ml / 0.5 oz)
- Sparkling water: 1 cup (240ml / 8.45 oz)
- Ice cubes: as needed

Directions:
Introduction: A cool and refreshing drink perfect for hot days.
Preparation: Muddle cucumber slices and mint leaves in a glass.
Mixing: Add lime juice and top up with sparkling water.
Assemblage: Fill the glass with ice cubes and stir gently.

Nutritional Information (per serving):
Calories: 10 kcal, Fat: 0g, Carbs: 2g (0.07 oz), Protein: 0g, Sodium: 5mg, Potassium: 40mg, Phosphorus: 5mg

Storage: Best served immediately.

Presentation: Serve in a highball glass with a mint sprig.

Variations: Add a splash of ginger ale for a spicy twist.

212. BRITISH BERRY FIZZ

Preparation Time: 5 minutes
Servings: 1

Ingredients:
- Fresh blueberries: 1/4 cup (40g / 1.41 oz)
- Fresh raspberries: 1/4 cup (30g / 1.06 oz)
- Sparkling water: 1 cup (240ml / 8.45 oz)
- Ice cubes: as needed

Directions:
Introduction: A fizzy, berry-filled delight that's both tasty and hydrating.
Preparation: Muddle the blueberries and raspberries in a glass.
Mixing: Fill the glass with ice cubes and top up with sparkling water.
Assemblage: Stir gently to combine.

Nutritional Information (per serving):
Calories: 20 kcal, Fat: 0g, Carbs: 5g (0.18 oz), Protein: 0g, Sodium: 5mg, Potassium: 40mg, Phosphorus: 5mg

Storage: Best served immediately.

Presentation: Serve in a mason jar with a straw.

Variations: Use mixed berries for a different flavor profile.

213. GINGER APPLE REFRESHER

Preparation Time: 5 minutes
Servings: 1

Ingredients:
- Apple juice: 1/2 cup (120ml / 4.23 oz)
- Fresh ginger, grated: 1/2 tsp (2g / 0.07 oz)
- Sparkling water: 1/2 cup (120ml / 4.23 oz)
- Ice cubes: as needed

Directions:
Introduction: A revitalizing drink with the zing of ginger and the sweetness of apple.
Preparation: Add grated ginger to apple juice and mix well.
Mixing: Pour the mixture over ice in a glass and top up with sparkling water.
Assemblage: Stir gently to combine.

Nutritional Information (per serving):
Calories: 50 kcal, Fat: 0g, Carbs: 13g (0.46 oz), Protein: 0g, Sodium: 5mg, Potassium: 50mg, Phosphorus: 5mg

Storage: Best served immediately.

Presentation: Serve in a tumbler with a ginger slice.

Variations: Add a splash of lemon juice for extra tanginess.

214. CITRUS HERBAL ICED TEA

Preparation Time: 10 minutes
Servings: 2

Ingredients:
- Herbal tea bag: 1
- Boiling water: 1 cup (240ml / 8.45 oz)
- Orange juice: 1/4 cup (60ml / 2.11 oz)
- Lemon juice: 1 tbsp (15ml / 0.5 oz)
- Honey: 1 tsp (5ml / 0.18 oz)
- Ice cubes: as needed

Directions:
Introduction: A refreshing herbal iced tea with a citrus twist.

Preparation: Steep the tea bag in boiling water for 5 minutes. Remove the tea bag and let it cool.
Mixing: Add orange juice, lemon juice, and honey to the cooled tea and stir well.
Assemblage: Fill two glasses with ice cubes and pour the tea mixture over.

Nutritional Information (per serving):
Calories: 40 kcal, Fat: 0g, Carbs: 10g (0.35 oz), Protein: 0g, Sodium: 5mg, Potassium: 30mg, Phosphorus: 5mg

Storage: Can be refrigerated for up to 2 days.
Presentation: Serve in a glass with a slice of lemon.
Variations: Use lime juice instead of lemon for a different flavor.

215. MINT AND LIME SPARKLER

Preparation Time: 5 minutes
Servings: 1

Ingredients:
- Fresh mint leaves: 6-8
- Lime juice: 2 tbsp (30ml / 1 oz)
- Sparkling water: 1 cup (240ml / 8.45 oz)
- Ice cubes: as needed

Directions:
Introduction: A simple yet refreshing drink with the zest of lime and freshness of mint.
Preparation: Muddle the mint leaves in a glass.
Mixing: Add lime juice and fill the glass with ice cubes.
Assemblage: Top up with sparkling water and stir gently.

Nutritional Information (per serving):
Calories: 10 kcal, Fat: 0g, Carbs: 2g (0.07 oz), Protein: 0g, Sodium: 5mg, Potassium: 10mg, Phosphorus: 5mg

Storage: Best served immediately.
Presentation: Serve in a highball glass with a lime wedge.
Variations: Add a splash of lemonade for a sweeter version.

216. LOW-ALCOHOL PIMM'S CUP

Preparation Time: 5 minutes
Servings: 1

Ingredients:
- Pimm's No. 1: 30ml (1 oz)
- Lemonade: 1/2 cup (120ml / 4.23 oz)
- Fresh cucumber slices: 2
- Fresh strawberry slices: 2
- Fresh mint leaves: 4-5
- Ice cubes: as needed

Directions:
Introduction: A classic British summer drink made with a lower alcohol content.
Preparation: Fill a glass with ice cubes.
Mixing: Add Pimm's No. 1 and lemonade.
Assemblage: Garnish with cucumber, strawberry slices, and mint leaves.

Nutritional Information (per serving):
Calories: 80 kcal, Fat: 0g, Carbs: 10g (0.35 oz), Protein: 0g, Sodium: 10mg, Potassium: 30mg, Phosphorus: 5mg

Storage: Best served immediately.
Presentation: Serve in a tall glass with a straw.

Variations: Add a splash of soda water for a lighter version.

217. RENAL-FRIENDLY GIN AND TONIC

Preparation Time: 5 minutes
Servings: 1

Ingredients:
- Gin: 30ml (1 oz)
- Low-sodium tonic water: 1/2 cup (120ml / 4.23 oz)
- Cucumber slices: 2-3
- Lemon slice: 1
- Ice cubes: as needed

Directions:
Introduction: A classic gin and tonic tailored for those with kidney concerns.
Preparation: Fill a glass with ice cubes.
Mixing: Add gin and top up with low-sodium tonic water.
Assemblage: Garnish with cucumber and lemon slices.

Nutritional Information (per serving):
Calories: 90 kcal, Fat: 0g, Carbs: 5g (0.18 oz), Protein: 0g, Sodium: 5mg, Potassium: 10mg, Phosphorus: 5mg

Storage: Best served immediately.
Presentation: Serve in a highball glass.
Variations: Add a few fresh mint leaves for a refreshing twist.

218. WHISKY AND GINGER

Preparation Time: 5 minutes
Servings: 1

Ingredients:
- Whisky: 30ml (1 oz)
- Ginger ale: 1/2 cup (120ml / 4.23 oz)
- Lime wedge: 1
- Ice cubes: as needed

Directions:
Introduction: A simple, yet flavorful cocktail featuring whisky and ginger ale.
Preparation: Fill a glass with ice cubes.
Mixing: Add whisky and top up with ginger ale.
Assemblage: Squeeze the lime wedge over the drink and drop it in.

Nutritional Information (per serving):
Calories: 100 kcal, Fat: 0g, Carbs: 10g (0.35 oz), Protein: 0g, Sodium: 5mg, Potassium: 10mg, Phosphorus: 5mg

Storage: Best served immediately.
Presentation: Serve in a rocks glass.
Variations: Use diet ginger ale for a lower-calorie option.

219. LAVENDER LEMONADE

Preparation Time: 10 minutes
Servings: 2

Ingredients:
- Fresh lavender sprigs: 2
- Lemon juice: 1/4 cup (60ml / 2.11 oz)
- Honey: 1 tbsp (15ml / 0.5 oz)
- Sparkling water: 1 cup (240ml / 8.45 oz)
- Ice cubes: as needed

Directions:

Introduction: A floral and refreshing lemonade, perfect for relaxing afternoons.
Preparation: Steep lavender sprigs in 1/4 cup of boiling water for 5 minutes. Remove the sprigs and let it cool.
Mixing: Combine lavender water, lemon juice, and honey, and stir well.
Assemblage: Fill two glasses with ice cubes and top up with sparkling water.

Nutritional Information (per serving):
Calories: 40 kcal, Fat: 0g, Carbs: 10g (0.35 oz), Protein: 0g, Sodium: 5mg, Potassium: 20mg, Phosphorus: 5mg

Storage: Best served immediately.
Presentation: Serve in a glass with a lavender sprig.
Variations: Use lime juice instead of lemon for a different flavor.

220. STRAWBERRY BASIL MOCKTAIL

Preparation Time: 5 minutes
Servings: 1

Ingredients:
- Fresh strawberries, sliced: 1/4 cup (40g / 1.41 oz)
- Fresh basil leaves: 4-5
- Lemon juice: 1 tbsp (15ml / 0.5 oz)
- Sparkling water: 1 cup (240ml / 8.45 oz)
- Ice cubes: as needed

Directions:
Introduction: A refreshing mocktail with the sweetness of strawberries and the freshness of basil.
Preparation: Muddle strawberries and basil leaves in a glass.
Mixing: Add lemon juice and fill the glass with ice cubes.
Assemblage: Top up with sparkling water and stir gently.

Nutritional Information (per serving):
Calories: 15 kcal, Fat: 0g, Carbs: 3g (0.11 oz), Protein: 0g, Sodium: 5mg, Potassium: 20mg, Phosphorus: 5mg

Storage: Best served immediately.
Presentation: Serve in a mason jar with a basil leaf.
Variations: Add a splash of orange juice for extra sweetness.

221. SPICED APPLE MOCKTAIL

Preparation Time: 5 minutes
Servings: 1

Ingredients:
- Apple juice: 1/2 cup (120ml / 4.23 oz)
- Cinnamon stick: 1
- Cloves: 2
- Sparkling water: 1/2 cup (120ml / 4.23 oz)
- Ice cubes: as needed

Directions:
Introduction: A warm and spiced drink, perfect for cozy evenings.
Preparation: Heat apple juice with cinnamon stick and cloves in a small pan until warm. Let it cool and remove the spices.
Mixing: Pour the spiced apple juice over ice in a glass and top up with sparkling water.
Assemblage: Stir gently to combine.

Nutritional Information (per serving):

Calories: 50 kcal, Fat: 0g, Carbs: 13g (0.46 oz), Protein: 0g, Sodium: 5mg, Potassium: 40mg, Phosphorus: 5mg

Storage: Best served immediately.

Presentation: Serve in a glass with a cinnamon stick.

Variations: Use pear juice instead of apple for a different flavor.

Cooking Strategies

Cooking healthily is crucial for those with kidney problems. Using the right cooking techniques can help further reduce the sodium, phosphorus, and potassium content in your meals. Here are some handy tips:

Low-Sodium Cooking Techniques

1. Steaming:
   - Steaming preserves nutrients without adding salt. Try flavouring your steamed vegetables with fresh herbs, garlic, or a squeeze of lemon juice.

2. Grilling and Baking:
   - Grilling or baking foods instead of frying them reduces the need for salt. Marinate meats and fish with spices, herbs, and citrus juices before cooking to add flavour without extra sodium.

3. Light Sautéing:
   - Lightly sauté vegetables in olive oil with spices, avoiding high-sodium sauces or condiments. Use garlic, onions, and chilli to add flavour.

4. Boiling and Double Boiling:
   - Boiling vegetables and discarding the water can help lower their potassium content. For a greater reduction, try double boiling by changing the water halfway through cooking.

Reducing Phosphorus and Potassium

1. Ingredient Choices:
   - Opt for foods low in phosphorus and potassium. For example, use cauliflower and zucchini instead of potatoes and spinach.

2. Pre-Treating Foods:
   - Peel and cut vegetables into small pieces and soak them in water for several hours before cooking to help reduce potassium content.

3. Rinsing Canned Foods:
   - Rinse canned beans and vegetables under running water to reduce sodium content.

4. Using Low-Phosphorus Substitutes:

- Use rice or almond milk instead of regular milk. Substitute high-phosphorus cheeses with lower-phosphorus alternatives like ricotta.

General Tips

1. Spices and Herbs:
   - Use fresh herbs and spices to flavour foods. Parsley, basil, thyme, rosemary, mint, and coriander are great salt substitutes.

2. Low-Sodium Broths:
   - Make homemade broths using fresh bones and vegetables, avoiding store-bought versions that often contain high levels of sodium.

3. Portion Control:
   - Keep portions of meat and fish small and balance with plenty of low-potassium vegetables. This helps control overall phosphorus intake.

More Tips for Eating Out

Eating out can be a challenge for those with kidney issues, but with some smart choices, you can enjoy tasty and healthy meals. Here are some tips on what to eat in British restaurants:

Common Dishes in British Restaurants

1. Fish and Chips:
   - Opt for grilled fish instead of fried and ask for it to be prepared without salt. Replace chips with a side of grilled vegetables or a low-potassium salad.

2. Roast Dinner:
   - Ask for a smaller portion of roast meat and choose low-potassium sides like cauliflower, carrots, and courgettes. Avoid gravy or request a low-sodium version.

3. Full English Breakfast:
   - Choose low-sodium options like boiled or scrambled eggs without salt, turkey bacon, and replace baked beans with grilled mushrooms.

4. Curry:

- Many restaurants offer curries with various meat and vegetable options. Request a low-sodium version and choose plain rice instead of naan or fried bread.

5. Soup and Sandwich:
  - Opt for soups made with vegetable broth without added salt and sandwiches with low-sodium ingredients like grilled chicken and fresh vegetables. Avoid high-sodium cheeses and sauces.

Strategies for Eating Out

1. Ask for Modifications:
  - Don't hesitate to ask for modifications to menu items. Restaurants are often willing to adjust recipes to accommodate dietary needs.

2. Avoid Pre-Made Dishes:
  - Choose dishes that are made to order rather than pre-prepared ones, as it's easier to request no added salt or lower phosphorus and potassium ingredients.

3. Control Condiments:
  - Request sauces, dressings, and condiments on the side, so you can control the amount you use and opt for low-sodium options.

4. Drink Moderation:
  - Limit beverages high in phosphorus and potassium like fruit juices and sodas. Opt for water or unsweetened tea.

5. Plan Ahead:
  - If possible, check the menu online before going to the restaurant. This allows you to make informed choices and prepare any special requests.

By following these cooking strategies and tips for eating out, those with kidney problems can enjoy delicious and safe meals both at home and in restaurants, keeping sodium, phosphorus, and potassium levels in check.

INDEX

All-purpose flour 78; 80; 81; 101; 102; 103; 104; 105; 107; 108; 109; 110; 111; 112; 113; 114
Almond extract 104; 114
Almond milk 28; 29; 31; 32
Apple juice 28; 120; 124
Apples 34; 35; 36; 64; 69; 101
Arborio rice 47; 49
Asparagus 26; 61
Asparagus spears 26
Aubergine 73; 90
Avocado 14; 18; 85; 89; 93
Bacon 22
Bagels 25
Baking powder 16; 18; 19; 27; 101; 102; 103; 104; 107; 108; 109; 110; 111; 113; 114
Baking soda 104; 105; 107; 110; 112
Balsamic glaze 94
Balsamic vinegar 60; 66; 71; 74; 87; 89
Banana 18; 29; 30; 32
Basil 47
Beef roast 39; 41
Beef steak 50
Beef stew meat 37; 40
Beetroots 60
Bell pepper 90
Bell peppers 45; 48; 61; 68; 73; 90
Berries 17
Black beans 45
Black pepper 14; 18; 21; 23; 24; 25; 26; 37; 38; 39; 41; 42; 43; 44; 45; 46; 48; 50; 51; 52; 53; 54; 55; 56; 57; 58; 59; 60; 61; 62; 63; 64; 65; 66; 67; 68; 69; 70; 71; 72; 73; 74; 75; 76; 77; 78; 79; 80; 81; 82; 83; 84; 85; 86; 87; 88; 89; 90; 91; 92; 93; 94; 95; 96; 97; 98; 99; 100
Black pudding 78
Blue cheese 92
blueberries 14; 15; 88
Blueberries 14; 15; 28; 29
Boiling water 121
Bran flakes 19
Bread crumbs 117
Broccoli florets 96
Brown rice 45
Brown sugar 102; 105; 111; 112; 113
Brussels sprouts 60; 66

Butter 15; 16; 17; 18; 19; 20; 21; 24; 25; 27; 56; 63; 64; 65; 66
Butternut squash 59
Canned tuna in water 85
Capers 25; 56
Carrot 29; 53; 82; 83; 98
Carrot juice 29
Carrots 34; 37; 39; 47; 66; 68; 70; 76; 79; 81; 95; 96; 98
Cauliflower 45; 59; 77
Cauliflower florets 117
Celeriac 65
Celery 37; 42; 47; 95; 96; 99
Cherry tomatoes 14; 22; 62; 70; 87; 89; 94
Chicken breast 37
Chicken sausages 22
Chickpea flour 79
Chickpeas 46; 115
chopped 24; 26; 29; 30; 31; 33; 34; 37; 38; 39; 40; 41; 42; 43; 44; 45; 47; 48; 51; 53; 54; 55; 56; 57; 58; 59; 62; 63; 65; 66; 67; 68; 69; 70; 72; 73; 74; 75; 76; 77; 79; 80; 81; 83; 84; 85; 86; 87; 88; 89; 90; 91; 93; 95; 96; 98; 99; 100
Chopped cilantro 61
Ciabatta bread 62
Cinnamon 20; 24; 34
Cinnamon stick 124
Coconut milk 31; 32; 46
Cod fillets 41; 55
Cooked barley 36
Cooked beetroot 67; 88
Cooked beets 34
Cooked black beans 61
Cooked chicken breast 93
Cooked crab meat 85
Cooked quinoa 61
Cooked roast beef 92
Corn 45; 61
Corned beef 38
Cornish hens 52
Cornmeal (polenta) 108
Cornstarch 37; 40; 44
Cottage cheese 14; 22
Courgette 26; 90
Courgettes 73; 79

Creamy peanut butter	114
crumbled	78; 87; 88; 89; 91; 92
Crumpets	20
Cucumber	22; 29; 30; 35; 68; 71; 85; 87; 89; 119; 122
Cumberland sausage	38; 40
Cumin	51
Curry powder	43; 46
Dark chocolate chips	112
Dijon mustard	64
Dill	22; 25; 43; 54; 57
Dried herbs (basil, oregano)	60
Dried oregano	117
Dried thyme	117
Duck breasts	52
Egg	18; 19; 27; 40; 41; 51; 53; 59; 78; 80; 81; 102; 111; 112; 113; 114
Eggplant	47; 48
Eggs	21; 22; 24; 25; 26; 27; 43; 101; 103; 104; 105; 106; 107; 108; 109; 110; 111; 114
Elderflower cordial	119
English muffins	21; 22
Extra virgin olive oil	67; 68; 69; 70; 71; 72; 73; 74; 75; 76; 77; 78; 79; 80; 81; 82; 83; 84; 86; 87; 88; 89; 90; 91; 115
Flour	16; 18; 19; 40; 41; 45; 59
Fresh arugula (rocket)	92
Fresh asparagus	72; 74
Fresh basil	62; 71
Fresh basil leaves	71; 73; 87; 91; 94; 123
Fresh blueberries	102; 120
Fresh chives	86; 93; 118
Fresh coriander	70; 76; 85; 90; 93; 98
Fresh coriander leaves	70
Fresh cucumber slices	121
Fresh dill	68; 84; 85; 87
Fresh ginger	34; 98; 120
Fresh herbs	56; 58
Fresh lavender sprigs	123
Fresh lemon juice	69
Fresh mint	29; 30; 33; 35; 67; 69; 76; 91; 95
Fresh mint leaves	29; 30; 33; 35; 67; 69; 76; 95; 119; 121
Fresh mozzarella balls	94
Fresh or frozen peas	69
Fresh parsley	55; 69; 72; 75; 80; 81; 85; 88; 90; 95; 96; 99
Fresh raspberries	102; 120
Fresh rocket (arugula)	86
Fresh rosemary	73; 90; 115
Fresh sage leaves	100
Fresh spinach	83; 88; 92; 99
Fresh strawberries	123
Fresh strawberry slices	121
Fresh thyme	57; 68; 74; 80; 95; 97
Fresh watercress	67
Freshly ground black pepper	115; 116; 117; 118
Frozen peas	75; 95
Garlic	46; 48; 49; 51; 53; 55; 56; 57; 58; 60; 62; 73; 77; 79
Garlic powder	46; 51; 57; 60; 116
Gin	122
Ginger ale	122
Granola	15
Granulated sugar	101; 102; 103; 104; 106; 107; 108; 109; 110; 111; 112; 113; 114
Grapes	15
Grated beetroot	108
Grated carrots	105
Grated Parmesan cheese	117; 118
Greek yogurt	15; 28; 29; 30; 31; 32; 33; 34; 35; 36; 43; 57; 68; 86; 87
Green apple	30
Green cabbage	69
Ground beef	53
Ground cinnamon	101; 104; 105; 111
Ground coriander	78
Ground cumin	78; 79; 96; 98; 117
Ground ginger	103; 110
Ground nutmeg	105
Ground turkey	51
Haddock fillets	42; 43; 55
halved	14; 21; 22; 23; 45; 52; 60; 62; 64; 66; 70; 77; 87; 89
Ham	21
Herbal tea bag	120
Honey	14; 15; 23; 28; 29; 31; 32; 33; 34; 35; 36; 102; 121; 123
Ice cubes	28; 29; 30; 31; 32; 33; 119; 120; 121; 122; 123; 124
Juniper berries	53
Kale	66
Kippers	57
Kiwi	33
Lamb	40; 51
Large mushrooms	58
Lean beef mince	82
Lean lamb mince	83

Lean minced pork	80
Leek	95
Leeks	37; 64; 75; 99
Lemon juice	18; 29; 30; 42; 43; 44; 45; 51; 54; 56; 57; 58; 64; 67; 68; 69; 70; 72; 85; 86; 87; 88; 91; 102; 107; 113; 121; 123
Lemon slice	119; 122
Lemon slices	56
Lemon wedges	85
Lemon zest	41; 54; 55; 57; 61; 72; 74; 84; 102; 107; 113
Lemonade	121
Lentils	47
Lettuce leaves	93
Lime	56
Lime juice	85; 90; 93; 109; 119; 121
Lime wedge	122
Lime zest	109
Low-fat cheddar cheese	82; 92; 97
Low-fat cheese	19; 20; 27
Low-fat cream cheese	25; 83; 84; 86; 93
Low-fat feta cheese	88
Low-fat Greek yogurt	85
Low-fat milk	65; 97; 99; 100; 101; 102; 103; 104; 106; 107; 108; 109; 111
Low-fat ricotta cheese	73; 89
Low-fat yogurt	16; 17; 105; 108; 110
Low-sodium baked beans	19; 22; 25
Low-sodium breadcrumbs	78; 80
Low-sodium cheddar cheese	59
Low-sodium cheese	45; 46
Low-sodium chicken broth	37; 39
Low-sodium cocktail sauce	85
Low-sodium fish broth	42; 43; 44
Low-sodium ham	95
Low-sodium Hollandaise sauce	21
Low-sodium hummus	90
Low-sodium mozzarella	47
Low-sodium mustard	82
Low-sodium tomato sauce	47
Low-sodium vegetable broth	47; 48; 49; 75; 76; 77; 95; 96; 97; 98; 99; 100
Low-sugar granola	16; 17
Low-sugar jam	17; 20
Mackerel fillets	42; 58
Maple syrup	35
Marmalade	15
Marmite	17
Mashed potato	78
Melon	91
Milk	16; 18; 19; 21; 23; 24; 27; 40; 41; 81
Minced lamb	38; 39
Mini sausages	81
Mint	15; 51; 63
Mixed berries	16; 88; 110
Mixed spring greens (spinach, arugula, etc.)	70
Mixed vegetables	46; 48; 49
Mushrooms	22; 23; 27; 47; 83
Nutmeg	66
Oats	23; 38
Olive oil	14; 23; 26; 27; 37; 38; 39; 40; 41; 42; 43; 44; 45; 46; 47; 48; 49; 50; 51; 52; 53; 54; 55; 56; 57; 58; 59; 60; 61; 62; 63; 64; 65; 66; 116; 117; 118
Onion	26; 37; 38; 39; 40; 42; 46; 47; 48; 51; 53; 76; 77; 79; 83; 95; 96; 97; 98; 99; 100
Onions	45
Orange juice	29; 30; 108; 121
Orange zest	108
Oranges	67
Overripe bananas	104
Papaya	31
Paprika	46; 59; 79; 90; 116
Parchment paper	56
Parsley	41; 51; 54
Parsnips	63; 78; 97
Peaches	31
Pearl barley	95
Pears	35; 67; 86
Peas	39; 63; 66; 83
peeled	29; 30; 31; 32; 33; 34; 38; 41; 59; 60; 63; 64; 65; 67; 75; 76; 81; 85; 97; 99; 100
Pimm's No	121; 122
Pineapple chunks	32
Plaice fillets	56
Popcorn kernels	118
Pork chops	51
Portobello mushrooms	74
Potato	82; 83; 97; 99
Potatoes	26; 38; 39; 41; 44; 64; 75; 81
Powdered sugar	107
Prosciutto slices	91
Quail eggs	80
Quinoa	48
Rabbit legs	53
Radishes	68; 71; 87
Raisins	111
raspberries	88

Raspberries	28
Red bell pepper	26
Red cabbage	64
Red lentils	96; 98
Red onion	67; 68
Rice	14; 24; 43
Rice cakes	14
Ricotta cheese	58
Ripe tomatoes	71
Rolled oats	28; 34; 35; 36; 57; 102; 111
Rosemary	50; 53; 65
Saffron	49
Salmon fillets	43; 57
Salt	16; 18; 21; 23; 24; 115; 116; 117; 118
Scallions	59
Sea salt	60
Seabass fillets	56
Self-raising flour	106
Shredded cabbage	81
Shredded coconut	109
Sliced almonds	54; 104; 114
Sliced ham	93
Sliced turkey breast	92
Smoked haddock	25; 43
Smoked haddock fillets	25
Smoked mackerel fillets	86
Smoked paprika	117
Smoked salmon	25; 44
Smoked salmon slices	84
Sole fillets	45; 54; 56
Soy sauce (low-sodium)	48
Sparkling water	41; 119; 120; 121; 123; 124
Spinach	21; 27; 30; 32; 33; 58
Spinach leaves	30; 32; 33
strawberries	14; 15; 88
Strawberries	14; 15; 32
Strawberry jam	106
Sugar	19; 20; 24; 27
Swede (rutabaga)	64; 65
Sweet potatoes	59; 79; 117
Teacakes	17
Thyme	47; 48; 50; 52; 59; 63
Tomato	20; 46; 96
Tomatoes	23; 48; 77; 98
Trout fillets	54
Unsalted butter	101; 102; 103; 104; 105; 106; 107; 108; 109; 110; 111; 112; 113; 114
Unsweetened cocoa powder	107
Vanilla extract	104; 105; 106; 108; 110; 111; 112; 114
Venison steaks	53
Vinegar	25; 64
Walnuts	86; 89
Water	10; 23; 24; 25; 29; 30; 34; 35; 36; 37; 40; 44; 64
Water or ice	34; 35; 36
Watermelon chunks	30; 33
Whipped cream	106
Whisky	122
White fish fillets	41; 44
Whole chicken	50
Whole wheat wraps	21
Wholemeal baguette	92
Wholemeal bread	15; 17; 18; 19; 20; 22; 24; 25; 26
Wholemeal bread slices	82; 86
Wholemeal crackers	84
Wholemeal flour	27
Wholemeal pastry	83
Wholemeal pie crust	37; 40
Wholemeal shortcrust pastry	82
Worcestershire sauce	53; 54
Worcestershire sauce (low-sodium)	82
Yogurt	51
Zucchini	48; 60; 68; 91; 116
Zucchini, chopped	68

Printed in Great Britain
by Amazon